MW01627481

STRAIGHT FROM THE HEART

A Torah Perspective on Mothering Through Nursing

Written by

Tehilla Abramov

and

Malka Touger

Based on Tehilla Abramov's lecture series on mothering through nursing

TARGUM / FELDHEIM

First published 1990

ISBN 0-944070-18-3

Phototypeset at Targum Press

Published by:
Targum Press Inc.
22700 W. Eleven Mile Rd.
Southfield, Mich. 48034

Distributed by:
Philipp Feldheim Inc.
200 Airport Executive Park
Spring Valley, N.Y. 10977

Distributed in Israel by:
Nof Books Ltd.
POB 23646
Jerusalem 91235

Printed in Israel

לעילוי נשמת

אבי מורי

ר׳ **ישראל אלכסנדר** ב״ר **חיים בן ציון**

כץ ז״ל

נלב״ע ט״ו אדר תשמ״ה

ת.נ.צ.ב.ה.

This book is dedicated
to my mother
in deep appreciation.

May she continue to be a source
of growth and inspiration
ad meah v'esrim shanah.

Rabbi CHAIM P. SCHEINBERG
KIRYAT MATTERSDORF
PANIM MEIROT 2.
JERUSALEM, ISRAEL

הרב חיים פנחס שיינברג
ראש ישיבת "תורה אור"
ומורה הוראה דקרית מטרסדורף
ירושלים טל. 521513

The great privilege of being a "Mother in Israel" is often unappreciated in our generation. Such alien concepts as family planning and career women have conspired to relegate mothering to the status of old-fashioned sentimentality.

It is therefore a pleasure to welcome the publication of *Straight from the Heart* by Mrs. Tehilla Abramov. This is an excellent presentation of the timeless values which the Torah has placed on motherhood. It marshals an impressive array of recent studies reflecting the discovery made by modern medicine and psychology of the practical wisdom imparted to us by Chazal regarding the woman's role as mother.

Following in the path of its predecessor, *The Secret of Jewish Femininity,* this book is calculated to make the Jewish woman proud of bringing children into this world, lavishing motherly love upon them in physical and emotional ways, and raising them to be Torah Jews through the special natural gifts with which Heaven has endowed her.

It is my *tefilah* that Mrs. Abramov, who has been so successful in influencing an entire generation towards a greater awareness of Taharat Hamishpachah as the secret of marital happiness, will also succeed through this book in heightening an appreciation of the gift and potential of motherhood. May her words, written in a style that speaks to the modern reader, open the hearts of all present and future mothers to the honored privilege of raising their beloved children in the ways of the Torah.

Chaim Pinchus Scheinberg

Rabbi Chaim Pinchus Scheinberg

RABBI S. WASSERMAN
PONIM MEIROT 15/10
MATERSDORF, JERUSALEM
ISRAEL (02) 537-420

הרב שמחה וסרמן
רח' פנים מאירות 15/10
מטרסדורף - ירושלים

Dear Mrs. Abramov:

Congratulations on the publication of your newest book, *Straight From the Heart,* to light up the role, joys, happiness, and fulfillment of Motherhood.

When Moshe Rabbeinu was ordered to offer the Torah to the Jewish People (Exodus 19:3), he was to address the Jewish women first. The Midrash explains that this was in order that they raise their children in Torah. The future of our people is in the hands of Jewish mothers. You have the *z'chut* to light the way for Jewish motherhood in the darkness of contemporary society.

Concerning the midwives during the Egyptian exile, we read, "as the midwives feared G-d, they kept the children alive" (Exodus 1:17). Rashi comments that because of their actions, they were blessed to count among their descendants Moshe Rabbeinu, Aharon Hakohen, King David and Moshiach (ibid. 1:22).

May all those concerned with Jewish motherhood and childbirth have the merit of speeding up our redemption and the coming of the Moshiach.

Rabbi Simcha Wasserman

Rabbi Simcha Wasserman
Jerusalem

הרב ישראל גנס

רח' פנים מאירות 2

קרית מטרסדורף, ירושלים 94 473

טלפון 531782

The book *Straight from the Heart,* which discusses the Jewish outlook on motherhood and nursing, has been presented to me. The book is written by Mrs. Tehilla Abramov, who also authored *The Secret of Jewish Femininity.*

I have checked the *halachot* cited in this book, and have found them worthy of publication.

The contents of this book will undoubtedly benefit the Torah public, inspiring the Jewish mother to carry on her age-old tradition of complete devotion to her loftiest task—that of "a Mother in Israel."

Yisrael Ganz

What has gone wrong with motherhood in our time? Bearing children and raising them have become such frightening responsibilities, and maternal love has become such a favorite target of satire and scorn: the generation gap has replaced the silver cord.

It is therefore a pleasure to welcome the publication of *Straight From the Heart* by Tehilla Abramov, an analysis of the Jewish approach to mothering with its accent on nursing and showing motherly love. It offers sensible down-to-earth guidance in how to rediscover the joys of motherhood.

In her earlier work, *The Secret of Jewish Femininity*, the author expertly delineated a Torah perspective on how a woman could find total fulfillment in her G-d given role as a woman. Her new, informative and interesting book takes the woman a step further into fulfilling the special role she has been assigned by Heaven as the source and nurturer of human life.

Much of the book, as its subtitle indicates, is dedicated to the nursing aspect of motherhood. The reader will soon learn that nursing is not merely a biologically superior avenue of nutrition, but a relationship between mother and child which carries on where the umbilical cord leaves off.

The author is uniquely qualified to write on this subject. She has addressed international conferences of prenatal care and has counseled countless individuals on this subject. Now her insights and experience are available for the general public through this timely work which indeed speaks to a generation of present and future mothers "straight from the heart."

Mendel Weinbach

Rabbi Mendel Weinbach, Dean
Ohr Somayach Institutions
Jerusalem

ב"ה

shaare zedek medical center מרכז רפואי שערי צדק

Mrs. Tehilla Abramov,

It is with great pleasure and enthusiasm that I endorse the publication of the much needed book entitled *Straight from the Heart*.

Those of us who have dedicated our professional lives to the care of the newborn and the strengthening of the biologic bond between the mother and the child cannot help but respond in a most positive way to the content of this instructional manual. Not only is the information regarding the critical role that breast feeding plays in the health of the infant and mother presented in a most clear, comprehensive and scientifically accurate manner, so too is the spiritual and religious value of this natural technique emphasized.

As such, both from the perspective of a pediatrician who specializes in the care of newborns and infants and as a committed Jew who sees our heritage supportive of what is best for infant care, let me congratulate you on your success in publishing this most welcome volume.

Sincerely yours,

Professor Arthur I. Eidelman MD FAAP
Director, Department of Neonatology
Shaare Zedek Medical Center
Jerusalem

Acknowledgments

My thanks to:

— Mrs. Malka Touger, whose creative writing skills have enabled this book to emerge;

— Mrs. Sarah Shapiro for her most capable editing of the manuscript;

— all the wonderful mothers whose authentic experiences appear in this book and who serve as an inspiration to us all;

— all those whose encouragement was the force which made this book a reality.

With heartfelt gratitude to *Hashem Yisborach,*

Tehilla Abramov
Kislev 5750

Table of Contents

When nursing her newborn child for the very first time, a mother should begin on the left side.

(*Tzava'at Rabbi Yehudah HaChasid*)

...because the baby should have his first meal from the place that's closest to the seat of understanding—the heart.

(*Knesset Chachmei Yisrael* 914)

Chapter One
Loving Your Baby

It was one of those serene moments that a mother treasures. I sat relaxing on the couch. With one arm I cradled my baby, who had contentedly fallen asleep after nursing, and with the other I held my toddler, who was "reading" a story to me. The older children were busily transforming their fantasies into Lego reality. A deep sense of satisfaction stirred within as I recalled David HaMelech's words: "Happy is the mother of children."[1]

This mother's experience is shared by thousands of other Jewish women the world over. She and her children feel a unique bond with each other. Their relationship with her has all the durability, intensity, and depth it needs to carry them through the myriad challenges that will arise during their childhood and adolescence.

When God instructed Moshe Rabbeinu to transmit the Torah to the Jewish people, He told him: "Thus you shall say to the house of Yaakov and tell the children of Yisrael."[2] Our Sages explain that "the house of Yaakov" refers to the women:

---

1. *Tehillim* 113:9.
2. *Shemot* 19:3.

Moshe was instructed to teach the Torah to the women first because "they introduce their children to the study of the Torah."[3]

The Torah of the Mother

The Mishnah[4] discusses the different stages of a child's education. A five-year-old begins Chumash; a ten-year-old begins Mishnah; a thirteen-year-old becomes obliged to observe the commandments; a fifteen-year-old begins the study of Gemara... And the Rema[5] rules that "as soon as a child reaches the age of three, one teaches him to read in order to prepare him for learning Chumash."[6] Thus, we can see from the sources that "education" commences with the learning of Chumash at the age of five, or perhaps with the learning of "aleph bet" at the age of three. Yet schoolteachers and rebbes are usually responsible for these aspects of the education of a child, so what is the role that mothers play when they "introduce their children to the study of Torah"?

It would appear that this is referring to the period from birth up to the age of three, a time that Rav Shimshon Raphael Hirsch calls the nursing years: "Mothers start worrying about the education of their children too late. They do not utilize the best period of time for preparing a child for formal education. They let the most vital time for *chinuch* in a child's life slip by them, and when they finally try to devote themselves to educating the child, they have already lost most of the chances to ensure a successful education... In my opinion, the most important period for education is that time when true *chinuch* is most often ignored, a period of time

---

3. *Shemot Rabbah* 29:2.
4. *Avot* 5:25.
5. Rema, citing Abarbanel in his commentary on *Avot*.
6. *Shulchan Aruch, Yoreh De'ah* 245:8.

when education is deemed not possible—the first years of a child's life—the nursing years."[7]

This theme is echoed in *Alei Shor*: "Education begins from the moment a baby is born. A tiny infant perceives much more about his environment than we adults attribute to him. This early confrontation with his surroundings influences his behavior and his developing personality. His experiences even as a wee baby become an integral part of his being."[8]

Shlomoh HaMelech declares: "Listen, my son, to the counsel of your father, and do not forsake the Torah of your mother."[9] A father generally focuses his counsel on particular behavior, imparting specific aspects of knowledge to his child. In contrast, a mother's guidance is all-embracing. "The Torah of your mother" encompasses a wide range of educational experiences that make Torah an essential part of a child's being. It is the mother who educates her child in the most fundamental ways, gearing his development towards reaching his utmost potential and laying the foundation for a life of Torah and mitzvot.

It is because of this vital role that mothers play in the education of their children that our Sages advise: If one wants upright children one should marry an upright woman."[10] This "upright woman," explains the Meiri, is a woman who knows how to educate her children in Torah, *middot*, and correct behavior.

A mother, therefore, has a great part in her child's successes and achievements. When the book of *Melachim* summarizes the Jewish rulers' accomplishments, it often cites the monarch's name together with that of his mother, acknowledging that it was the "Torah of his mother" that started him on the path to greatness.

---

7. Shimshon Raphael Hirsch, *Yesodot HaChinuch* vol. 2, pp. 44-45.
8. *Alei Shor, Ma'amar HaChinuch*, p. 263.
9. *Mishlei* 1:8.
10. *Niddah* 70a.

What is the "Torah of his mother" that is so vital to the development of the child and is best taught during the nursing years? Our Sages give us one concrete example. When Rav Yochanan ben Zakai wished to praise Rav Yehoshua ben Chananiah, he declared, "Praiseworthy is she who bore him."[11] Our Sages stress that it was Rav Yehoshua ben Chananiah's mother who shaped her son's character. She would sit near the *beit midrash* with her tiny child so that the sounds of the students studying Torah would reach his ears. Is it any wonder, then, that Rav Yehoshua developed his unique potential for Torah scholarship—immersing himself in the familiar verses that had lulled him to sleep as an infant?[12]

The "Torah of his mother," as exemplified by the mother of Rav Yehoshua, whose example has been followed by Jewish women throughout the ages, obviously refers to something much more encompassing than one specific act. The "Torah of his mother" taught to the child during his nursing years is indeed all-encompassing: it is the Torah that we teach through "mothering." And to ensure that she is well-prepared for her vital role, God created woman with an extra dimension of understanding.[13] Thus, her natural instincts and sensitivity equip her well to forge and maintain the mother-infant bond.

The Mother-Infant Bond

> *Shortly after my first child was born, my great aunt came to stay with us for a few weeks. She harbored a lot of doubts concerning my approach to mothering.*
>
> *"Come now, Leah," she would say. "Do you really believe that a small baby absorbs all that attention? Why,*

---

11. *Avot* 2:8.
12. Jerusalem Talmud, *Yevamot* 8b.
13. *Bereishit Rabbah* 18:1.

he's such a tiny little thing, his senses are so limited and unaffected by his surroundings! Besides, with all that extra mothering, he'll never grow up to be independent!"

Holding my peace, I patiently acknowledged her genuine concern for my baby, explaining my perspective as clearly as I could.

Despite our difference of opinion, my great aunt's visit provided many enjoyable moments for all of us, and for my baby as well, though I do confess to heaving a sigh of relief when she left.

During my son's childhood, my great aunt visited frequently, mentioning often how nicely my independent, creative, outgoing son was developing. She made no further comments about my mothering of his siblings.

A few weeks prior to my son's bar mitzvah, I received a card from my great aunt.

"My dear niece," she wrote, "as your son's big day approaches, I remember when he was quite small; it seems like only yesterday. As he embarks upon adulthood, I recall your devoted care for him in infancy.

"What I condemned as smothering has proven to be supreme mothering. What I disapproved of as enveloping was actually developing. What I thought was an excessive bind turned out to be an impressive bond.

"I'm sure that when he thanks all the rabbis and teachers in his bar mitzvah speech, he won't forget to thank you!"

Long before pediatricians began to take note of mother-infant bonding, Shmuel, a practicing physician in Talmudic times, proved this point convincingly. The Talmud describes an experiment he conducted. A group of women stood in line handing an infant one to another. Among them was the child's mother, who was instructed to act no differently than the other women. Shmuel followed the infant's facial expressions and body movements as he was being passed around. He noticed a demonstrative response in the baby as he was held by his mother.[14]

Selma Fraiberg, professor of child psychoanalysis at the University of Michigan Medical School, has conducted extensive research on the ties a baby develops from the very beginning of infancy to the end of his first year.[15] She has noted an obvious, consistent preference for the parents, and, in particular, the mother, the primary figure in the first years of life.

Her study documents the infant's responses to his mother and calls them "love language." The smiles, the gurgling, the intense grip of tiny fingers holding on for dear life, are some of the ways the baby communicates in this special language.

The human smile is innate, the universal greeting of our species. Even in the early weeks of life it appears in deep sleep (and let no well-informed observer convince you that it is "just gas"!). Gradually, the smile is elicited more and more frequently by external stimuli. Between the ages of three and six months, a baby smiles more—and more joyfully—at his mother than at anyone else. It is to his mother that he babbles and coos, and it is her embrace that he seeks. The mother's care for her baby creates a bond that teaches him to discriminate between her and other people. This is a positive development, though well-meaning friends and relatives may disapprovingly attribute it to "too much pampering." On the contrary, this attachment constitutes the foundation for the child's healthy future development.

> *My four- and six-year-old boys were playing out in the front yard late one summer afternoon. Suppertime had arrived and I called them in. No answer. Raising my voice, I called again. Still no response. I walked out to the porch*

---

14. *Ketubot* 60a.
15. Selma Fraiberg, *How a Baby Learns to Love* (La Leche League International, reprint no. 123, June 1979).

calling my sons' names, searching for them, but they were nowhere in sight.

Although I do not consider myself a nervous mother, my heart was pounding. My imagination got the better of me and I began thinking of all the terrifying things that might have happened to my children.

Before I had a chance to contemplate my next move, I was startled by a loud "Boo!" followed by hysterical laughter. There were my two little pranksters crawling out of their hiding place.

"Oh! You naughty boys!" I scolded, hugging them at the same time. "I was so worried when I couldn't find you. Please don't scare Mommy like that again!"

Later, I sat nursing my baby. Her tiny fingers curled tightly around my own, as if reassuring herself that Mommy would not leave her. I recalled the experience I had had that afternoon. I, an adult, had become shaky when my boys "disappeared." Obviously, they couldn't have wandered far. I should not have been so frantic and should have realized that they would show up in no time.

"And yet," I thought to myself, "if my baby cries when I leave the room I expect her to use her 'better judgment' and 'understand' that Mommy is not disappearing forever...."

Fear of Separation

As the baby's attachment to his mother grows, he increasingly fears separation from her. Between his sixth and twelfth month he exhibits a behavioral change commonly referred to by specialists as the "stranger reaction."

"I don't know what has gotten into him," apologized a perplexed mother to her mother-in-law, who had just arrived from out of town. "He used to be so friendly to everyone."

On her last visit three months ago, the baby's grandmother had enjoyed cuddling, rocking, and singing to him—and he had responded beautifully. Now he showed no sign of recognition and burst into tears at her every attempt to touch him.

This baby's strange behavior is really not strange at all. It is a perfectly normal response and it reflects a strong, healthy mother-infant bond. The baby is making a simple yet profound statement: "My mother is the center of my world, and this stranger—an intruder—has invaded the intimacy of my private universe."

After rejecting the advances of a newcomer, the baby's eyes search the room for his mother. When he finds her, his frown turns into a smile. This is his overture to be picked up, a healthy sign that the baby has learned a lesson in love. Love is exclusive. The baby is telling his mother that she is the only one who really matters to him. Just as a loving couple grieves upon separation, so the baby is anxious about his separation from his mother. He has come to recognize her as the special person in his life, the prime source of joy and comfort, the satisfier of hunger, the protector: the most indispensable human being in his world.

If the baby's need to be secure and loved is met, he will learn that his relationship with his mother is not threatened by outsiders or by temporary separation. He will become more tolerant of strangers and learn to cope with his mother's absence. A mother need not force "maturity" upon her child out of fear that he'll become "overly attached." She needn't push him away when he longs for her reassurance. Her baby is learning a lesson in love and trust that will last him a lifetime, for the security felt by an infant leads to openness in responding to other people in the future.

The Lesson of Love

Love is a distinctly human need, and it offers unique rewards. It is natural for the person who offers this satisfaction and pleasure to become valued above all other persons.

Our Sages were well aware of a child's need for his mother and saw nothing unnatural in this need. The Mishnah[16] rules that a child who does not need his mother is obligated to sleep in a sukkah, implying that a child who does need his mother is not so obligated. The Gemara explains that a child who "needs his mother" is one who cries for his mother when he wakes up at night and continues crying until his mother comes. A child who "does not need his mother" is one who may cry out when he wakes up, but who will not persist with the crying if his mother does not appear. Our Sages saw nothing wrong either with a child crying specifically for his mother or with a mother responding to her youngster's need for attention—day or night.

In the course of research into mother-infant bonding, one study was carried out in an institution where this vital component of baby care was lacking.[17] The institution's shoestring budget allotted one caretaker to every fifteen or twenty babies in a ward, and the infants were bathed, fed, and changed by a rotating staff. Even the most loving nurse could hardly supply the foundations for bonding because of the heavy workload. The babies spent mealtimes, the most appropriate hours for much-needed human contact, lying alone in their cribs with propped up bottles. Indeed, the infants spent most of the day confined to their cribs.

Close comparisons were made with a control group of babies being raised by their natural mothers. In the first stages of the study, the institutionalized babies grew and manifested the

---

16. *Sukkah* 2:8.

17. Fraiberg, La Leche League International (hereafter referred to as LLLI), reprint no. 123, pp. 2-3.

natural desire for communication. By three months, they were smiling and babbling in response to human contact, albeit less than those in the control group.

The most dramatic difference occurred after three months. Among the babies in the institutionalized group, there were no signs of discrimination and preference for one caretaker; they reacted indifferently to everyone. The "stranger reaction" was lacking. There was no difference in the quality of their contact with their daily nurses and attendants, and that with occasional visitors, researchers, and observers. Everybody had equal value in the babies' eyes.

There were other differences between the babies raised in the institution and those in the control group. The infants cared for by their mothers demonstrated obvious displeasure and even distress when they lost sight of their mothers, even if they had merely left the room. In contrast, the institutionalized babies showed no grief in the absence of their caretakers. The pain felt upon separation is an expression of a baby's love. Because these infants lacked such a bond, they felt no pain.

All of us—even as adults—need someone to love. For an infant, constant motherly love is as vital to growth and development as sunshine is to a growing plant. A mother's loving bond with her baby will convince the child that his world can be a gratifying, rewarding place to be. The absence of such love imbues him with a sense that the environment is unsatisfying, unloving, and even hostile.

As the institutionalized babies got older, they achieved only a restricted range of sounds, and the speech development of those children who remained in the institution for an extended period was severely retarded.

This devastating evidence is hardly surprising. Communication is dependent upon the ongoing presence of human partners with whom to share vocal exchange. For a young child, there is no more stimulating partner than his loving mother, frequently at his side, communicating with him as she tends to his physical needs.

Rav Shimshon Raphael Hirsch makes the following telling comment: "A child takes the father's family name (as indeed the wife does), yet the language a child speaks is called his 'mother tongue' because it is his mother who devotes herself to him and communicates with him, developing his emotions in his formative years. Only afterwards does the father take over and develop the child's opinions about society and his function in this world."[18]

Follow-up studies of the babies who remained in the institution offer some disturbing insights into the effects of love starvation. Lacking the attachment and security of the mother-infant bond, these children had much difficulty learning to trust others. Since they had never experienced bonding and loving, many of them were unable to maintain stable relationships as adolescents.

Unfortunately, the lessons in love that a mother teaches her child were never transmitted to these children. The mother-infant bond, perpetuated, nurtured, and developed during those vital early years, lays the foundation for healthy interpersonal relations in the future. Rabbi Chaninah, one of our Sages, is quoted in the Talmud as saying that the care that his mother gave him in childhood stood him in good stead in old age.[19]

The power of human love is also mentioned by Ashley Montagu,[20] who describes a shocking report published by Dr. Henry Chapin in 1915. Dr. Chapin disclosed that, in a survey of ten orphanages in the U.S., with only one exception none of the babies lived to celebrate their second birthday.

In the wake of that study, a well-known American doctor visited a children's institution in Europe to compare approaches

---

18. *Yesodot HaChinuch*, vol. 2, p. 71.
19. *Chullin* 24b.
20. Ashley Montagu, *The Humanization of Man* (World Pub. Co., 1962).

to child care. He discovered far fewer fatalities in the European clinic. He also noticed the frequent presence of a woman who did not seem to be part of the staff. "Who is that 'mama'?" he asked, half jokingly, pointing to the big, jolly-looking woman balancing two babies on her well-padded hips.

"Oh! That's Ol' Anna," replied the head nurse. "She's been around here for years. Whenever everything we've done for a baby has failed, we turn him over to Ol' Anna. She's always successful."

Subsequently, the doctor hired women to fill the role of "Ol' Anna" in all the American institutions in which he worked, with encouraging results. The European clinic had stumbled upon what was later documented scientifically. By 1920, many pediatricians were implementing this vital lesson, instructing their staff to pick up, amuse, and cuddle the babies several times a day.

Loving by Giving

Today, the importance of the mother-infant bond has been universally recognized. However, the extent and quality of the mother's influence depends on her effort and her commitment to mothering. A mother's love for her tiny infant is natural, but how far she goes to develop that love and its healthy expression is up to her.

This is not always easy. When we give love to adults, we usually receive in return, yet when we love children, we sometimes end up feeling that we're the only ones doing the giving. Furthermore, a baby's simple physical needs often overshadow the emotional aspects of the relationship. How does a mother express her love for her child? Not only through the contact they share, but also through the day-to-day chores that baby care involves.

Making a commitment to mothering is in itself an expression

of love. The Hebrew word for love, *ahavah,* is related to the word *hav*—"give." Giving is an expression of loving; and the more one gives, the greater the love. Loving by giving is an everyday (often all day!) practice for which God has endowed mothers with unique emotional resources. He has given us the potential to give of ourselves, our time, and our entire being.

The train from Kovno to Vilna was crowded and noisy. In one car sat a young man looking nervous and irritable. Across from him sat a quiet, distinguished-looking older man. When the older man opened the window a little wider to air out the compartment, the young man reprimanded him rudely: "Must I freeze because of you?" The older gentleman politely apologized and closed the window completely. Again and again the young man found something the old man did to complain about, glowering at his neighbor throughout the journey.

When the train arrived in Vilna, the young man was surprised to see a large crowd gathered on the platform. "Whom have you come to greet?" he asked someone as he got off the train.

"Why, don't you know? That man who just came out of this very compartment is Rabbi Yisrael Salanter!"

The young man's face turned ashen. He realized that he had insulted a saintly man for no reason and felt deeply ashamed. Unable to find peace, he resolved to apologize to the rabbi at the earliest opportunity.

When the young man entered Rabbi Yisrael's hotel room, the sage greeted him warmly. Before he had a chance to apologize, Rabbi Yisrael asked him, "Have you been able to rest after the train ride?"

Struggling to speak through his sobs of remorse, he begged the rabbi for forgiveness, but was not given a chance to finish.

"Surely I forgive you," Rabbi Yisrael smiled. "There's no

need to dwell on the subject. Tell me, my son, what is your name? Where have you come from and what is the purpose of your trip? Do you have proper food and lodging?"

The young man introduced himself, explaining that he had come to Vilna to become a shochet, a ritual slaughter.

Rabbi Yisrael's face lit up. "I'll be more than happy to help you achieve your goal," he offered graciously. He proceeded to make all the necessary arrangements for the young man's enrollment in a shechitah program, and throughout the following year, Rabbi Yisrael spared no effort assisting him. Like a devoted father, he convinced the yeshiva authorities to offer the young man a second exam after he failed the first and personally tutored him until he could pass it. Afterwards, he arranged a job for him in a nearby town.

Needless to say, the young man was overcome with gratitude and love for the kindly rabbi who had gone out of his way to help him. Before leaving for his new job, the young man approached Rabbi Yisrael to thank him and bid him farewell.

"Please, Rabbi, I would like to understand why you have bothered so much with me. I was grateful enough when you forgave me for insulting you on the train. Why did I merit all this extra care and attention?" he asked humbly.

Rabbi Yisrael took his hand and looked at him with loving eyes. "I wanted to be sure that I had forgiven you with all my heart. Besides, are we not commanded to love our fellow man?"

As Rabbi Yisrael's behavior indicates, giving not only expresses love but enhances it. Constant giving requires much effort and forces us to rise above self-concern. As a person learns to give, he or she develops a different perspective on life, and long-term goals and values become more important than immediate gratification. A love relationship becomes not just a temporary joy but a lifetime bond.

The mother-child relationship is the classic example of how a bond of love can be enhanced by giving. The constant effort which a mother invests in caring for her child creates a relationship that will only be strengthened by the passage of time.

The challenge presented by such a commitment is not beyond the capacity of any woman. Mothers are blessed with the natural ability to give. It is no coincidence that the Hebrew term *rachamim*, mercy, shares the same root as the word *rechem*, womb. During her pregnancy, a mother grows not only physically but emotionally, expanding her potential to give generously of herself. After the child is born, she continues to nourish, nurture, and rear him, loving by giving and creating a bond that will last a lifetime.

It is this quality of Jewish femininity that has been passed on from generation to generation, from mothers to daughters, linking today's mothers with our matriarchs. Sarah, Rivkah, Rachel, and Leah were prophetesses renowned for their insight, propagators of the Jewish faith, and partners in their husbands' endeavors. With all these distinguished attributes, the title they are endowed with is: mother.

In the spirit of the heritage transmitted by our matriarchs, every Jewish home is a training center for future parents. Much of the know-how and sensitivity that a woman needs in order to master the art of mothering is taken from her own mother's example. Each mother serves as a model for her own children to follow when they reach parenthood. As one married daughter wrote to her mother in the concluding paragraph of a long letter:

> *"My dear Ima, did you know that during all the time that you were building your own home, you were also building mine...?"*

In Hebrew, a homemaker is referred to as the *akeret habayit*. This phrase can also be interpreted as *ikro shel habayit*, the essence of the home, implying that she is the one who sets the tone and the spirit of the home environment. The Jewish woman makes a Jewish home more than just her family's abode.

God's command to the Jewish people to build a sanctuary, "And you shall make Me a sanctuary, and I will dwell within them,"[21] raises a question. Why doesn't the Torah say "I will dwell within *it*"? By stating the command in this manner, God teaches us that the Divine Presence is not confined to the sanctuary alone. Every Jewish home is "a sanctuary in microcosm."

The priests in the Temple were constantly occupied with the daily chores of the Temple service. Though the ultimate goal of the sacrificial offerings, the *korbanot*, was to draw the people close to God, these sacrifices involved such seemingly mundane activities as cleaning the ashes off the altar. Similarly, when a woman busies herself with all the chores required to maintain her household, she must realize that her house is a dwelling place for God.

The Temple was also a house of prayer. A woman must realize that her efforts need *siyata dishmaya*—the help of God. The unique skills with which she has been endowed, of giving with love and loving by giving, must always be accompanied by her prayers to God that He bless her tremendous efforts.

When the saintly Chafetz Chaim was an old man, someone brought him his mother's old, worn-out prayer book. With glistening eyes, the great sage clutched the treasure lovingly and said: "It was the prayers my mother uttered over this tear-stained siddur, its pages tattered from being turned by trembling fingers, that brought blessings upon her family."

---

21. *Shemot* 25:8.

Chapter Two
Mothering Through Nursing

"And the woman sat and nursed her son until he was weaned."[1]

After years of longing for a child, Chanah was finally blessed with a baby. When the time came for their pilgrimage to Shilo to give thanks to God, Chanah asked her husband, Elkanah, to be excused from the journey as long as her baby was still nursing.

"Do as you see fit; remain here until he is weaned,"[2] replied her husband.

What a profound sense of gratitude Chanah must have felt to God, who at last had answered her prayers. Yet she recognized her immediate priority—to stay home and nurse her infant—and did not accompany her husband on his pilgrimage of thanksgiving.

Such was the motherly devotion of Chanah, mother of the prophet Shmuel, a leader whom our Sages equate with Moshe Rabbeinu and Aharon HaKohen.

---

1. *I Shmuel* 1:23.
2. ibid.

The Mitzvah of Mothering

The story of Chanah the prophetess provides us with the model of a woman who viewed mothering as her highest priority, who refused to do anything which she believed would in any way disturb the mitzvah she was involved in, the mitzvah of "mothering." Chanah understood that she was educating her son. These were "the nursing years," the years when Shmuel was receiving the "Torah of his mother," the years when the mother-infant bond was being cemented and Shmuel was learning the lessons of love and devotion. The fulfillment of this mitzvah of mothering overruled the fulfillment of the mitzvah of *aliyah leregel*.[3]

Nursing is Natural

When praying for a son, Chanah implored God: "You have not created anything without a purpose. You have given me breasts, were they not intended to nurse a child? Give me a baby so I may use Your creation."[4] Nursing is the ideal vehicle for the expression of mothering; there is no better practical way of forging the mother-infant bond.

When our matriarch Sarah was ninety years old God allowed her to conceive. An extraordinary event certainly, and yet there was still another dimension to this miracle. After bearing a son, Sarah resumed lactating and nursed him for two years. All the people marveled: "Who would have ventured to say that Sarah would nurse babies?"[5] Our Sages ask: Wasn't bearing a child at the age of ninety miraculous enough? We know that God does not perform a miracle in vain. Why the additional miracle of nursing? Perhaps the fact that Sarah resumed lactating and nursed her child was not an additional

---

3. *Meam Loez, I Shmuel* 1:22.
4. *Brachot* 31b.
5. *Bereishit* 21:7.

miracle "in vain"—it was part and parcel of the miracle of Sarah giving birth. Nursing a baby is an intrinsic part of birth.

The Hebrew word for a baby is *yonek*—"one who nurses." Describing a baby in this manner gives us insight into the importance of nursing. Sucking is an automatic reflex of a newborn, and for some time after birth, a baby "sees through his mouth." Nursing is the natural expression of the baby's dependence on his mother.

When God created woman and gave her the power to reproduce, He also provided her with the means of nourishing her newborn. Nursing is simple yet remarkable. Superbly designed to meet the physical needs of both mother and baby, nursing enhances and strengthens the mother-infant bond. A baby's dependence on his mother creates in her the urge to give to him; thus, the more dependent a baby is on his mother, the more he will receive from her.

After giving birth to her first child, one woman wrote to a friend:

> *Aside from being natural for the baby, nursing is quite natural for mothers, too. I am amazed at the simple physiological fact that women who have given birth are automatically supplied with the breastmilk with which to nourish their babies. Our relationship is so close that the sound or even the thought of my baby can bring on my need, and my desire, to nurse her.*

A woman's breasts were formed in the most appropriate area of the body, close to her heart.[6] A child cradled in his mother's arms, nestling his head where he can hear the soothing rhythm of her heartbeat, can surely sense that along with milk, he is receiving love.[7]

---

6. *Brachot* 10a.
7. *Knesset Chachmei Yisrael* 914.

Our Sages emphasize this point, commenting on the dramatic difference between human and animal nursing. Animals lack the contact a human baby receives in his mother's loving arms. An animal's teats are located on the lower half of the body; her young suckle while facing her rear end. In contrast, a human baby is held near the heart and looks upon his mother face to face.[8]

The Far-Reaching Effects of Nursing

In times gone by, hiring a wet nurse was a widespread practice even among less than affluent women. Why then did Sarah, mother of Yitzchak Avinu, and Chanah, mother of Shmuel HaNavi, not avail themselves of this convenience? A mother's nursing of her children goes far beyond providing for their physical needs. It is, as we have seen, an act of *chinuch.* When Pharaoh's daughter rescued a tiny crying infant afloat in a basket on the Nile, she summoned one Egyptian wet nurse after another, but the infant refused them all. On the advice of the baby's sister, Pharaoh's daughter agreed to try a Jewish wet nurse for the child. It was only when the Egyptian princess called for the righteous Yocheved, the baby's mother, that the baby who was to become Moshe Rabbeinu sated his hunger. Rashi states that it was not fitting that the mouth which would in the future speak to the *Shechinah* nurse from a woman who had eaten non-kosher food, since her milk would also be affected.[9] (It is customary, therefore, that when a non-Jewish woman must nurse a Jewish child, she is told to eat only kosher food.) How profound an effect do we see in the act of nursing—an effect that lasts a lifetime!

Another incident that took place some two thousand years ago sheds more light on the profound effects of nursing. The

---

8. *Vayikra Rabbah* 14:3.
9. *Sotah* 12b.

Midrash tells how a non-Jewish wet nurse saved the life of one of the greatest rabbis of the time, Rabbi Yehudah HaNasi. The Romans had issued a terrible decree forbidding the Jews of Eretz Yisrael to perform circumcision on newborn sons. If they disobeyed, both parents and baby were to be put to death. Despite the decree, Rabban Shimon ben Gamliel and his wife had their son circumcised. The Roman ruler suspected them and ordered both parents and son to Rome immediately, to stand trial before the Emperor.

It was a long hard journey for the woman nine days after childbirth and for little Yehudah. On the way, they stopped, exhausted, to rest at the home of a friendly Roman couple whom they knew. The couple had themselves just had a baby, whom they named Antoninus. Upon hearing the sad plight of their Jewish friends, Antoninus' mother suggested that they switch babies for a short while. "You take my baby, who is uncircumcised, and show him to the Emperor. And so your lives will be saved. I will care for your baby in the meanwhile."

The two mothers made the switch and the trick worked. Rabban Shimon ben Gamliel, his wife, and little Yehudah were saved from certain death when the Emperor saw, to his amazement, an uncircumcised baby in his mother's arms. Subsequently, Antoninus grew up to become Emperor of Rome himself and a patron of the Jewish people. He and Rabbi Yehudah HaNasi retained their friendship throughout their lives. Ultimately, Antoninus was privileged to study Torah, and in his later years he underwent circumcision himself to become a *ger tzedek*, a righteous convert. The Midrash tells us that he merited inheriting both this world and the next world as a result of his having nursed from a righteous Jewish woman.[10]

Another story of the far reaching effects of nursing is told about Sarah Imeinu. When Yitzchak was weaned she made a

---

10. *Tosafot Avodah Zarah* 10b; *Menorat Hamaor* 83:2.

party for him, and there she nursed all the babies who came with their mothers,[11] thus proving she was in fact Yitzchak's mother at the age of ninety. The Midrash tells us about the effects of Sarah's milk on those babies: ali the babies who nursed from Sarah got great goodness. "They became good like Sarah because the good, blessed milk brought into their hearts the fear of Heaven."[12]

"Just as the book of life is opened for a newborn child at the beginning of his life, similarly is the book of education then opened to him. What is the title of the first chapter in the book of a baby's life?—'the drawing of nourishment.' What name shall we give to the first 'book of education'? Let us call it 'the chapter of overflowing love.' Who teaches the first chapter? The mother... A child's education is begun by his mother... and the first lesson she teaches him is that of love... He seeks nourishment for the hour but obtains nourishment also for the remainder of all his days. Such is the nourishment which a mother's love gives to her children. And in all the world, no love is greater."[13]

Our Sages, emphasizing the importance of the mother nursing as opposed to a wet nurse, record the following insight: "One who buys wheat from the market is compared to a baby whose mother has died and must be fed by wet nurses and is not satisfied... One who grows his own grain is likened to a baby who nurses at his mother's breasts."[14] Binyan Yehoshua explains that because the nature of the world is such that a woman was created to nurse her own child, she will normally be able to satisfy him.[15]

---

11. *Baba Metzia* 87a.
12. *Meam Loez, Vayeirah* 21:7.
13. Eliyahu Kitov, *The Jew and His Home* (New York: Shengold Pub. Inc., 1974) p. 202.
14. *Avot DeRabbi Natan* 31:1.
15. ibid.

The Baby's Dependence

Another insight into the nursing relationship was brought out by one nursing mother's personal experience.

> *My grandmother had suffered a stroke and was recuperating in a rest home. The doctors explained that from a purely physiological perspective, she had a fairly good chance of resuming many of her former activities. "However," they explained, "the greatest asset in recuperation from a stroke is positive thinking and willpower."*
>
> *My grandmother, unfortunately, had neither. Totally shattered by her sudden paralysis, she was unable to summon any inner strength or determination. So my brothers and sisters and I all became engaged in the attempt to lift her spirits and dispel her pessimism. We each had our assigned hours to spend with her so as to provide her with constant support.*
>
> *One day, as I was preparing to take my turn at the rest home, the phone rang. "Hello," said Becky, my babysitter. "I'm terribly sorry I wasn't able to call earlier, but I can't make it today."*
>
> *There was no time to call anyone else; as it was, I was running late. Besides, the chances of finding an available babysitter on the spur of the moment were virtually nil.*
>
> *I made up my mind quickly. Fastening my little girl in her car seat, I set out for the drive. "It's all for the best," I told myself. "Seeing the baby might give Grandma lift. And it's not a hospital, so I don't have to be anxious about germs and possible contamination."*
>
> *My grandmother could barely find the strength to greet us with a smile. We spent the next hour in a one-sided conversation, with me doing all the talking. Occasionally, she would sigh or shake her head, but this was her only response. She wasn't physically incapable of responding, she was just overcome with depression and self-pity.*

By this time, my baby had become quite fidgety, making it obvious that she wanted to nurse. I realized with a start that I wasn't "dressed for the occasion." I hadn't planned on nursing, and the back-buttoned dress I was wearing was hardly suitable.

Suddenly, my grandmother perked up, sensing that she could help. "You can wear one of my robes," she offered, and I did so, gratefully. Pulling the curtain closed around my grandmother's bed, I settled down to nurse. As my baby latched on eagerly, my grandmother watched her great-granddaughter relax.

In the quiet moments that followed, my grandmother spoke up with a sudden spurt of energy. "Ruth, I was watching your baby during the entire time it took you to organize yourself for nursing. Though she was obviously anxious to nurse, she seemed to wait patiently, following you with trusting eyes, knowing that you would accommodate her desire. It's amazing. She's so dependent upon you, and she trusts you completely. Just look at that expression of satisfaction on her little face!"

"Grandma," I said softly, "aren't our lives dependent on God in just that way? He is surely worthy of our trust and faith. He is watching over you and He will help you recover."

She closed her eyes and nodded in affirmation. I knew by the look on her face that a load had lifted from her heart. For the first time she could imagine that, God willing, she was going to make it.

The constant involvement required by the nursing bond may prompt some women to think of nursing as too much of a bind. For the baby himself, however, this connection is a blessing, for "separation from his mother can cause severe anxiety in a baby."[16]

---

16. *Tosafot Rid Ketubot* 60a.

This observation was made centuries ago. Modern research, too, views separation of mother and infant as unnatural and undesirable. Psychologist Dr. Walter Barker, head of the Early Childhood Development Project at Bristol University, England recently rocked the medical establishment by urging parents not to leave babies alone at any time for the first four to six months of life. He says parents should carry them in a sling during the day and put them in or near their own beds at night![17]

During intrauterine life, an infant is completely contented, nourished by his mother for nine months.[18] Suddenly he is thrust out into the world—his first experience of separation. The sudden confrontation with his strange new surroundings is definitely a shock to his tiny being after having floated peacefully in his mother's protective womb. Is it any wonder that he voices his displeasure with loud shrieking? What a pleasure and comfort for the infant to find himself enveloped in his mother's arms and nestling at her breast.

> *Both of us, baby and I, cherish the time we share nursing. The demands of nursing discourage me from leaving him, which wouldn't be good for the baby anyway. Nursing is like his "insurance policy" against separation.*

Obligation and Privilege

The Mishnah lists breastfeeding her children as one of a wife's obligations towards her husband.[19] And that nursing was always considered the "natural" method of feeding a child can be seen from the *brachah* of Yaakov Avinu. In his desire to shower his beloved son Yosef with the ultimate goodness, the

---

17. *London Daily Mail*, 14 August 1989.
18. *Niddah* 30b.
19. *Ketubot* 59b.

expression he used was: "blessings of the breast and womb."[20]

A woman who nurses experiences the satisfaction of knowing that she's doing what is right and beneficial. This contributes to her peace of mind and tranquility, which are great emotional assets in strengthening the mother-infant bond.

Relaxation

The natural demands of nursing also compel the mother to physically relax: she must cease any strenuous activity and, in all likelihood, she'll take a seat.

> *My mother taught me a valuable lesson in conserving energy, which I adhere to religiously when nursing: "If you're standing, sit, and if you're sitting, lie down!"*

When a mother begins to nurse, her body produces a specific hormone that has a calming effect on her system, helping her to achieve a tranquil state. So whether she is gently rocking in a rocking chair or cushioned comfortably on the couch with her feet up, the nursing mother is able to stop, *relax*, and, of course, enjoy these special quiet moments that her nursing baby has "forced" upon her.

> *As I sit in my rocking chair nursing my baby, I gaze at that little face in real gratitude. Why, if not for his demands, I would never get these vital moments of peace in our constantly busy household.*

Sometimes babies force their mothers to relax and nurse them in the most awkward situations. One mother relates such an episode:

---

20. *Bereishit* 49:25.

One day I was driving on the interstate highway with my baby sleeping in the back seat. Suddenly, he woke up with loud crying. Hoping the movement of the car would lull him back to sleep, I continued driving. But it didn't work. I found it difficult to concentrate on the road and decided to stop and nurse him.

"NEXT EXIT—20 MILES," the road sign announced. I groaned. I could not go on driving like this. Though I knew it was illegal on this particular stretch of road, I found a safe spot and pulled onto the unpaved shoulder. Climbing into the back seat, I nursed the baby, who immediately, of course, stopped crying.

All went well until the very last moment. My baby was strapped into his seat, and I had turned on the ignition and flashed my left signal light, when a police car pulled up behind me. "Hey, lady! You can't stop on the freeway like that! That's a $100 fine."

My heart sank. "I'm terribly sorry, Officer. You see, my baby was crying and I had to stop and nurse him. Please understand."

It was only then that the policeman noticed the young passenger in the back seat. Peering through the window he was greeted with an enormous smile on my baby's face.

"Aw! What a cute little thing," the officer laughed. "I have a little fellow of my own at home. He doesn't take a bottle, huh? Well, neither does mine—my wife, why, she won't give him anything but her own milk. Gee, I know what it's like when they howl like that. Sometimes I think I could take along my little man and use him as a siren!"

The officer's face had softened. "All right, lady. I'll let you off this time, but don't let it happen again. And as for you, young man..." he wagged an accusing finger at my baby, "remember the law: drinking and driving don't mix!"

The Divine Gift

Just as the mother's body is optimally designed to facilitate the nurturing of her infant, so the infant's body is perfectly created to enable him to nurse. Even his physiological limitations are in accordance with this function. Research has determined that the distance at which the newborn has the best vision is exactly twenty-five centimeters. He cannot focus well on objects any closer or farther away. How wondrous is God's wisdom, for twenty-five centimeters is precisely the distance between a nursing baby and his mother's face! This remarkable yet often overlooked fact might be what prompted our Sages to suggest in the Midrash: "David HaMelech, while nursing as a baby, peered at his mother and glorified the Creator, singing: 'My soul pours out praises to God....'"[21]

Nursing a child is a great help in forging a strong mother-infant bond. The effects of that unique closeness are long-lasting and far-reaching.

> *Now that I am the mother of a teenager, I see that I'm reaping the benefits of the "loving by giving" process that involved me so deeply with my child when he was a baby. Those early years of bonding through nursing contributed immensely to our closeness, easing my daily confrontations with his growing, energetic, and demanding personality. I learned to "read" my son from infancy—his tendencies, preferences, whims, and moods. The foundation was being laid for mutual understanding and communication in the future without my really knowing it.*

Thus does the mother-infant bond bloom into the mother-child, mother-teenager, mother-adult closeness that lasts a lifetime. The connection we establish with our children during

---

21. *Tehillim* 103:1.

infancy creates a powerful foundation upon which a lifelong relationship can be built. We women are promised great reward[22] because the essence of our children's education is in our hands.[23] Nursing is a Divine gift that was bestowed upon us to help us succeed in the most challenging yet rewarding of human experiences—mothering.

Of course, many factors aside from nursing influence the quality of one's mothering, such as physical fitness, emotional peace of mind, and sensitivity to one's child, to name just a few. And as dedicated as a mother may be, she will be wise to remember that "everything is in the hands of Heaven."[24]

God created mothers with the capacity to nurse their children. But, as in most spheres of life, every rule has its exceptions. This surely applies when it comes to human development, for each person is an individual. Sometimes, finding an alternative manner of feeding is an absolute must. Under these circumstances, every effort should be made to provide the baby with as many of the benefits of nursing as possible, despite the use of a bottle, so that even when nursing cannot take place—nurturing can.

We offer the following helpful hints:

*When bottle feeding, approximate the nursing position as closely as possible—hold the baby in your arms, as opposed to propping him up with a bottle. Provide maximum skin contact, caressing and fondling while feeding in order to fulfill his vital need for maternal warmth.

*Prick small holes in the bottle nipple so feeding will take longer and baby will benefit from mother's closeness and touch all the more.

*Remember: though anyone can give a baby a bottle, frequent and extensive separation may have adverse effects

---

22. *Brachot* 17a.
23. Rav Eliyahu Vidash, *Reishit Chochmah*, part 3, chap. 42.
24. *Brachot* 33b.

on the baby (and on his mother). Minimize separation: there is no substitute for maternal love.

*If you must spend time away, a regular babysitter is preferable to a day-care center, where many babies are tended to by minimal staff.

Whatever her circumstances, a mother should provide maximum contact by holding the baby close to her during feedings and minimizing separations. With awareness and sensitivity, every mother can succeed in establishing a close mother-infant bond.

The nursing mother's quest for Divine blessing was expressed succinctly by the *anshei mishmar*—the men of stature who attended the offering of sacrifices in the Temple. They would pray "that expectant mothers give birth to full-term, healthy babies, and that lactating mothers succeed in nursing."[25]

Our Rabbis have suggested a prayer that nursing mothers themselves can recite, beseeching God to bless their good intentions and efforts:

> *May it be Your will, merciful God, that I have a plentiful milk supply for my infant. Bless me with sensitivity to his needs and let me not sleep heavily, so that when my baby cries my ears will open and I shall hear immediately. May I nurture him in health and joy....*[26]

---

25. *Taanit* 27b.
26. HaRav Eliyahu HaKohen, *Shevet Mussar*, chap. 24.

Chapter Three
More Than a Baby's Treat

While I was chatting at home with a friend over tea and cake, my twenty-two-month-old, who had been happily playing nearby, climbed up onto my lap and requested a "snack." Quite accustomed to this, I responded with a smile and proceeded to nurse him.

I could sense my friend's surprise at my nursing a toddler. The flow of conversation came to an abrupt halt. Somewhat embarrassed, she turned to my little one and blurted: "My, my, you seem to be enjoying yourself—what does it taste like?"

Without batting an eye, he replied matter-of-factly, "Just like honey!"

From the mouths of babes comes what sounds very much like the Torah's description of manna, the miraculous food that sustained the Jewish people in the desert for forty years.

Our Sages actually compare manna to breastmilk, for just as breastmilk tastes like any food the mother has eaten, so the manna tasted like any food the individual fancied.[1] Breastmilk is never boring, taking on the varied tastes of the different

1. *Yoma* 75a.

foods the mother has eaten during the day. This blessing of palatability plays an important role in the mother-infant bond. The baby relishes his time at the breast for the abundance of pleasure it affords his senses—the sweet smell and the delicate taste and texture of the breastmilk are so distinctive that a blind baby recognizes his mother by the smell and taste of her milk.[2]

The analogy to manna goes beyond taste, however. Just as the manna contained all the dietary components necessary to sustain the Jewish people, wholesome breastmilk provides baby with all his nutritional needs. In this chapter we take a closer look at its components and see why it is quite simply the most perfect food available for your baby.

Water

The proportion of soluble substances to water in breastmilk is perfectly balanced. Hydration and nourishment are accomplished harmoniously, never at each other's expense. Provided he gets enough breastmilk, a baby cannot dehydrate, and except under most unusual circumstances has no need for water.[3] (In case of extreme heat or if the child has a high fever, the mother must take every precaution to ensure that her child gets sufficient breastmilk—and that she herself drinks enough fluids to stimulate milk production.)

> *One sweltering summer day, my husband and I, our four children, and my brother- and sister-in-law hiked down a canyon towards the "Flour Cave" in Israel's Negev desert. Suddenly we discovered that our canteen was left behind.*
>
> *"We're almost there," I said as cheerfully as I could,*

---

2. *Ketubot* 60a.
3. Jan Riordan, *A Practical Guide to Breastfeeding* (St. Louis: The C.V. Mosby Co., 1983), p. 34.

knowing that to retrace our steps would take too long.

Finally arriving at the cave, my husband announced a short break before entering the dark tunnel that led through the cave. No one was more delighted with this delay than my ten-month-old daughter, who was strapped in a back-pack. For right there, in a dim corner of the tunnel entrance, I sat down to nurse her. "The older ones can wait," I thought, "but she really needs a drink."

My sunburned sister-in-law, quite unaccustomed to the heat, looked on enviously. "Boy! Am I jealous of little Dvori. She has a built-in canteen at her disposal!"

The winning comment, though, came from my eight-year-old son. The "Flour Cave" earned its name from the very soft, white limestone on its walls, which developed because of the dry climate and desert winds. Any slight contact with the limestone leaves one covered with "floury" sand. I must have been quite a "white sight" sitting there on a rock, leaning against the limestone walls.

"Mommy," my son exclaimed, pointing to the white coat of sand that covered me, "it's just like those babies in Egypt. Their mothers' hid them by the rocks, far away from the evil Egyptians who wanted to throw them in the Nile. We learned that Hashem sent angels to feed them!"

It was only as he burst out giggling that I realized I was the angel he was talking about.

Proteins

The proteins found in mother's milk help develop baby's brain cells and nerve endings, and protect him against disease and infection. These proteins, vital to the baby's growth, are easily and quickly digested, with almost no waste. Digestion is so efficient that a breastfed baby naturally requests shorter intervals between feedings than his bottle fed friend.

Since he utilizes all the protein in breastmilk, his stools are looser but their smell much less offensive.

Many a mother will attest to the bulkier stool and offensive smell of a bottle fed baby's diaper, evidence of undigested food elements.

Because it is geared toward bovine, and not human, development, cow's milk must be diluted and altered into formula for infants. Nevertheless, some elements remain that are simply unnecessary—and possibly counterproductive—for baby's growth. Further, the dilution process also takes out elements that are good for the infant!

Cow's milk contains three times as much protein as does breastmilk. This is quite an advantage for the calf, since its digestive system and growth pattern are perfectly designed to accommodate this ratio. Calves double their birth weight in two months. Babies, however, double their weight in six, and have no need for excess proteins. What's wonderful for the calf is less than ideal for the human child.

Thus, babies fed cow's milk based formulas are often (but not always!) heavier than their breastfed peers. Yet this is not a sign that they are healthier. Though the breastfed baby may eat more often yet weigh less than the bottle fed baby, the more complete utilization of the milk's nutrients is more important than weight gain.[4] A human infant must have the right nutrients so that his brain and nervous system develop properly—and those nutrients are found right there in breastmilk![5]

It is also important to note that different types of proteins are found in milk. One type, casein, which is found in much higher concentration in cow's milk than in breastmilk, forms a tough, rubbery curd that strains the digestive tract. Un-

4. La Leche League International, *The Womanly Art of Breastfeeding* (Franklin Park, Illinois: LLLI, 1981), p. 284.
5. ibid.

modified cow's milk can thus cause a baby much discomfort. Even in modified cow's milk, the protein curds take much longer to digest than in breastmilk. A bottle fed baby may thus go for longer intervals between feedings. This is not due to the superiority of cow's milk—quite the contrary! The curds formed in the baby's stomach simply take longer to digest and make baby feel full. In breastmilk, it is whey protein which predominates—a protein that is more nutritive and easier to digest.[6]

> *I envied my neighbor until I understood why her bottle fed baby went for four hours between feedings, while my nursing infant had no respect for clocks. When a nursing counselor explained the reason for this, I realized that superior feeding is better than easy feeding, and I resolved to postpone teaching my baby to tell time.*

Fats

Approximately forty percent of the caloric content of breastmilk consists of fats, which contribute significantly to the baby's development. As with the proteins, the baby absorbs these fats quickly and efficiently, thanks to breastmilk's enzymes.

Many of the fats in cow's milk, however, cannot be digested by baby at all. Not only do they pass through his system unutilized, they may actually rob him of his calcium supply in the process. Undigested fatty acids in cow's milk account for the foul odor when the baby regurgitates, while "breastmilk that a baby brings up is no more offensive than churned butter."[7]

It is obvious that the fat content in breastmilk is Divinely

---

6. Riordan, *A Practical Guide,* p. 30.
7. *Brachot* 63b.

designed to suit baby's needs. It is amazing that, in harmony with the baby's growth pattern, this fat concentration varies from week to week, from feeding to feeding, and even in the space of one nursing session.

The highest fat content is concentrated in the hind milk, which comes towards the end of a feeding.[8] (Thus, it is misleading to measure breastmilk's fat content based on a small sample, for it may not contain calorie-rich hind milk.) Therefore, to give her baby the full benefit of breastmilk, a mother should nurse until he shows he's satiated.

Carbohydrates

Providing energy for cell function, carbohydrates are present in both breastmilk and cow's milk—but in different proportions. Lactose, a milk sugar far more prevalent in breastmilk, benefits baby's growth immensely. Lactose enhances calcium absorption, metabolizes other milk sugars that supply energy to baby's rapidly growing brain, and helps prevent harmful organisms from settling in the intestines.

The high lactose concentration in breastmilk accounts for its sweetness. "The baby finds an assortment of sweet tastes in his mother's milk, thus enjoying every feeding and never tiring of it."[9]

The sugar in cow's milk must be increased for use in infant feeding. It is added to formulas sometimes in the form of lactose, other times in the form of sucrose or table sugar. While lactose breaks down and releases energy at a slow and steady pace, sucrose is released quickly into the blood, causing erratic fluctuations in blood-sugar level.

"In addition, since sucrose is sweeter than lactose, it seduces the baby away from breastmilk, just as chocolate milk

---

8. Riordan, *A Practical Guide*, p. 29.
9. *Tosefta Sotah* 4:1.

and other sweetened milks seduce the older child from regular cow's milk."[10]

Minerals and Salts

In breastmilk, the proportion of lactose to minerals and salt is perfectly balanced. In cow's milk, however, the low lactose content and high mineral concentration compel the baby's kidneys to work much harder processing this unsuitable combination of elements. This burden can overwhelm the digestive tract, upsetting the balance of fluids in the bloodstream.

Breastmilk contains more iron than cow's milk. In addition, up to fifty percent of the iron in breastmilk is utilized beneficially, in contrast to only four percent in cow's milk.[11] Breastmilk's higher levels of copper and vitamins C and E further contribute to efficient iron absorption. "A completely breastfed infant will maintain adequate iron stores up to twelve to eighteen months of age."[12] As a result, a totally breastfed baby becomes anemic much less often than his bottle fed peer. "Historically...breastfed infants have not been anemic."[13]

Higher levels of calcium, phosphorus, and magnesium are present in cow's milk than in breastmilk, although formulas generally try to reduce them somewhat. This excessive mineral content, unsuitable for infants, has been linked to several medical problems such as a certain type of muscular spasm, convulsions, and poor tooth enamel development followed by dental decay.[14]

---

10. LLLI, *The Womanly Art*, p. 287.
11. ibid., p. 289.
12. Sidney R. Kemberling, M.D., "Supporting Breastfeeding," *Pediatrics*, January 1979.
13. Ruth A. Lawrence, *Breastfeeding: A Guide for the Medical Profession* (St. Louis: The C.V. Mosby Co., 1985), p. 93.
14. Drs. Penny and Andrew Stanway, *Breast is Best* (London: Pan Books Ltd., 1981), p. 37.

Vitamins

As long as breastmilk is his major source of nourishment, a baby needs no vitamin supplements, provided that his mother is well nourished. It is she, rather than the baby, who must have a well-balanced, nutritious diet and may supplement her food intake with vitamins. A nursing mother who is properly nourished will be able to provide her baby, through her breastmilk, with all the nutrients he needs. (Remember, babies need sunshine as well for the production of vitamin D.) Says one medical authority: "Breastmilk alone is adequate for nutritional needs until the baby demonstrates an interest in table foods."[15]

Anti-Infection Factors

One of the most phenomenal features of breastmilk is its ability to ward off infection. In our sources it is written that one who wants to protect his child from illness should feed him his natural food—breastmilk.[16] Medically the reason is clear: breastmilk contains immunoglobulin, which carries antibodies against disease. During the first few months of life, a baby cannot manufacture antibodies against infection. He must depend totally upon the immunity he receives before birth from the placenta and after birth from his mother's milk. The anti-infection factors combine to fend off attacking organisms and promote the breastfed baby's optimum physiological functioning.

Cow's milk also contains antibodies. However, these antibodies protect against *animal* disease, and not necessarily against human ailments.

Boiling, freezing, and other means of processing render all antibodies impotent in both cow's milk and breastmilk.

---

15. Riordan, *A Practical Guide*, p. 32.
16. *Tzeidah Laderech*, section A:3.

Both calves and humans, therefore, thrive on fresh rather than processed milk.

In addition to the antibodies contained in breastmilk, the very act of breastfeeding minimizes the chance of infection. The milk flows directly from mother to baby, with very little contact with germs on the way. Skin bacteria are also reduced on the mother's areola (dark skin area) due to the workings of certain glands, whose antiseptic secretion acts as a natural disinfectant.[17] Regular showering will provide all the "natural sterilization" mother needs to nurse safely and comfortably.

Allergy Prevention

Due to the superior composition of breastmilk, it is obvious that babies *should* be breastfed. However, for the allergic baby, nursing becomes even more important.

> *"So, how's the baby?" inquired Dr. Schneider. He had good reason to ask. I had been a frequent visitor to his allergy clinic for years with my first three highly allergic children. This wasn't surprising; allergies run in both my husband's family and my own. We had spent many hours testing and subjecting my three little ones to excessive discomfort and anxiety, and eventually emerged with the longest shopping list of forbidden foods I'd ever seen. Feeding my children was one big ordeal.*
>
> *When my fourth baby was born, I considered breastfeeding. It had never crossed my mind that any connection existed between allergies and nursing till I came upon some magazine articles that strongly supported this view.*
>
> *"Whoever wrote this doesn't know my children," I thought wistfully, yet I decided to give it a try. Determined but skeptical,*

---

17. Riordan, *A Practical Guide*, p. 34.

I embarked on what was to be one of the most rewarding, enjoyable experiences in my mothering career.

So it was with much pleasure that I responded to the doctor's query. "Oh! Just fine, thanks."

"How are his allergic symptoms?" I could sense his surprise at my not having paid him one visit with the new baby.

"He doesn't have any."

"What in the world are you feeding him?"

"Dr. Schneider, I have found the best 'formula' ever. You see, we spent so much time and effort searching for the most suitable form of food for my highly allergic children. We looked for something nourishing, nutritious, non-toxic, gentle, easy on sensitive systems, palatable and on and on. I finally realized that what we were looking for was really me, a nursing mother."

Certain systems of proteins help prevent allergic reactions in the body. One of these, the IgA system, is not developed in infants until the age of six to nine months. If allergens (allergy inducing substances) enter the child's system before that time, problems can develop. If the body is given a chance to develop this IgA, allergic responses are much less likely. A baby who receives his mother's breastmilk receives an extra gift: his mother's IgA protein. This substance coats the body's intestinal lining, blocking undesirable foreign organisms from entering the bloodstream.

Many of the proteins in cow's milk can act as allergens. Though formulas are modified somewhat, these proteins are still present. Without a developed system to protect him, the baby can experience an allergic response.[18]

Not all allergic symptoms present themselves immediately.

18. Riordan, *A Practical Guide*, pp. 37-38.

The reaction may not surface until the next time the baby has cow's milk, or even later. "Unfortunately, a single bottle of cow's milk can sensitize a baby and so possibly cause allergic symptoms either at once, when he next takes cow's milk, or some time later."[19] A baby from an allergy-prone family is best protected by not being given even one bottle of formula. If the nursing mother must miss a feeding, she should express her own milk.

Allergic symptoms vary greatly, from diarrhea, vomiting, failure to thrive, anemia, eczema, coughing, and rattling of the chest to a wide variety of other negative reactions. The symptoms surface and disappear, and are often mistaken for viral infection. Many a mother has wondered "What caused them? Which treatment made them suddenly disappear?" Exclusive breastfeeding means peace of mind for the mother as she enjoys her nursing baby, blessed with the knowledge that she is doing the very best for her child.

Medical research has documented what nursing mothers have discovered through experience. In one study of children from allergy-prone families, fifty percent of the bottle fed babies developed eczema, versus only eight percent of the breastfed babies.[20] A survey carried out in Manchester in 1970 indicated that out of 170 infants hospitalized for gastroenteritis, only one (!) was breastfed.[21] Other studies have discovered that breastfed babies, after developing allergies when given supplemental foods, recover from the allergies when these foods are avoided, and are thus able to eat the foods at a later age without an allergic reaction.[22] And in a study carried out in 1978, Dr. E. Robbins Kimball, a pediatrician and member of La Leche League's professional advisory board, found that

19. Stanway, *Breast is Best*, p. 49.
20. ibid., p. 50.
21. ibid., p. 47.
22. LLLI, info. sheet no. 16, May 1975, p. 5.

the incidence of allergies is closely related to the length of time a baby is breastfed. "Nursing the baby [exclusively] for six months or longer provided the greatest protection from allergies."[23]

Sometimes an extremely sensitive baby may react to a substance in his mother's milk, such as the dairy products that she herself has eaten. In such a case, the solution is for the mother to eliminate the offensive food from her diet—not to panic and run for formula! That can only aggravate the sensitivity, not cure it.

In addition to its many nutritional advantages, breastfeeding offers other health benefits.

Mouth and Jaw Development

Breastfeeding encourages optimal mouth and jaw development. It does not unnaturally contort the baby's mouth and palate, and it exercises his cheek muscles, mouth, and tongue. When a woman breastfeeds, the nipple flexes its shape in the baby's mouth. The baby elevates and elongates the nipple, pushing it up against the hard palate with his tongue, while his gums and lips compress the areola. Besides enabling baby to get his food, this hard work helps prepare his tongue and mouth for proper speech and contributes to healthy facial development.

While breastfeeding is not a guarantee that the baby will never require orthodontia, since factors such as heredity also play their role, breastfeeding minimizes the likelihood of this problem. Bottle feeding, on the other hand, may very well increase it, because the rubber nipple pressing frequently against the roof of baby's mouth may narrow the upper dental arch, leaving less room for incoming teeth. In one survey

---

23. LLLI, *The Womanly Art*, p. 308.

of nearly five hundred children with such problems, only two had been breastfed.[24]

Prevention of Ear Infections

Of special interest is the role of breastfeeding in preventing one of the most common infant ailments—ear infections.

Bottle fed babies are more prone to ear infections. A breastfed baby, assisted by gravity and in control of his suction, regulates the milk flow. A baby who is fed lying down with a propped up bottle, however, has little control over the flow of milk, for it simply pours out into his mouth, whether or not he is ready to swallow. Further, excessive pressure created from sucking on the bottle may cause the milk to ooze into the middle ear, causing irritation or infection. Nursing at the breast does not require this kind of suction, so a breastfeeding mother can nurse lying down and not worry that this practice will cause an ear infection.[25]

> *With my first three children, whom I didn't nurse, I was in and out of the pediatrician's office with ear infections constantly. With Benny, I was determined to nurse, and my pediatrician hasn't "heard" from his ears at all!*

The Very Gift of Life

Breastmilk has given the very gift of life to some babies who could tolerate nothing else.

> *When my beautiful little girl was born, my joy was indescribable. We had waited so long for this baby and the miracle of her birth was overwhelming. My joy was much*

24. Stanway, *Breast is Best*, p. 55.
25. LLLI, *The Womanly Art*, p. 316.

mitigated, however, when I was suddenly gripped by an acute illness. Despite my utmost gratitude to God for blessing me with a child, I was saddened that I would not be able to nurse her, due to the medication upon which I was totally dependent. I could hardly believe that this was one of those rare situations in which breastfeeding was totally contraindicated.

My initial disappointment became a cause for serious concern when we found that my daughter could not tolerate milk or any milk-based formula. All other soy or meat formulas similarly caused diarrhea, vomiting, and extreme discomfort. My precious baby's life was in peril.

After many tests and experiments with alternatives, the doctors shook their heads in frustration, sadly acknowledging her pitiful appearance and dramatic weight loss.

"Our only suggestion is to try to obtain mother's milk for her," they told me.

On my own now, I was on the phone all day, knocking on doors, spreading petitions to save my baby's life. Quicker than I expected, salvation came from down the block: "Hello," said the pleasant voice on the telephone. "I heard about your baby. I'm a nursing mother with plenty of milk to spare and I will be happy to assist you."

This was the beginning of a wonderful friendship with the woman whose milk nourished my baby back to life and sustained her for her first year.

Since then, a "Milk Bank" has been formed in Jerusalem. A voluntary organization, it is the lifeline for many babies whose mothers are unable to supply them with breastmilk. These babies' lives are dependent upon it. I really felt proud after giving birth to my second child, whom I was able to nurse myself, that now it was my turn to be the "lifesaver." I was asked to express milk to sustain someone else's baby at the other end of the country.

Chapter Four
A Mother's Delight

After much reading and discussion I became convinced that nursing would be the best way to feed my baby. It was only after my "inauguration" into nursing, however, that I discovered just how beneficial breastfeeding was for me.

Though she might be well aware of the many advantages of breastfeeding, a woman may nevertheless overlook these blessings. Caught up in her other responsibilities, and seeking to fulfill her legitimate desire for intellectual and spiritual stimulation, social life, and personal development, she may not realize how much of an asset nursing really can be. All the demands of running her household, providing companionship to her husband, and educating her children, may "wean" her away from nursing. "There are so many daily practicalities I have to deal with," she might decide, "I have no time to even contemplate all those lofty ideals about breastfeeding!"

However, in many ways, nothing is more *practical* than nursing!

Convenience: Keeping Life Simple

The first benefit usually mentioned by nursing mothers is convenience. In our fast-moving yet comfort-oriented society, convenience is a major issue. What could be more convenient than breastfeeding? No need to prepare formulas, wash bottles, scrub nipples, or heat baby's meal. Mother's milk is sterile, readily available, and just the right temperature.

> *The convenience of nursing is a tremendous benefit, especially for night feedings. The baby's crib is right there next to my bed, so as soon as he stirs, I hear him and reach over to take him into my arms. I don't get out of bed and he doesn't get a chance to start howling. Then we both drowse off again as he nurses peacefully at my side. Even if I tuck him back into his crib when we finish, neither one of us really wakes up. In the morning I can't always be sure if I awoke during the night or not!*

A Reason To Relax

Another plus is the excuse breastfeeding provides to relax. Sitting or lying down to nurse is regarded by many a busy mom as time off. Often it's the only chance she gets to take a break from her hectic daily schedule.

While being "forced" to relax like this in a comfortable position, a breastfeeding mother can take advantage of her free hand, something bottle feeding does not permit. That extra hand can comfort an older child seeking attention, turn the pages of a book, hold a telephone receiver, write a letter, or even sip a drink (but beware of hot ones!).

Mobility

This is another unexpected advantage of breastfeeding. Trips, whether hiking or driving, are simplified, as all mother needs to pack for baby is herself! Nursing on a plane, train, or boat is easy and practical, allowing for more flexibility in the family's traveling plans.

Many a mom has been discouraged from going on vacation because of the hassles that accompany bottle feeding. It's no wonder, since she has to organize formula, containers, and bottles, all of which call for extra hand luggage. In addition, she must prepare, heat, and wash bottles while traveling.

As with adults, extensive driving and flying may cause baby discomfort and irritability, and he may react with total disrespect for his usual feeding schedule. The inconvenience of preparing yet *another* bottle while on a journey often leaves the distraught mother to deal with the annoyance of fellow passengers as well as a shrieking baby.

> *"Oh, no! Just my luck to be seated next to a lady with a baby," the woman muttered crossly as I located my seat on the plane. Smiling apologetically, I busied myself with organizing my baby and myself for the flight. The displeased look on her face made it quite clear that she would tolerate no disturbance. With a silent prayer in my heart, my baby and I snuggled close as we took off.*
>
> *It was a long, non-stop flight. Quietly and discreetly, every peep my baby made was quickly hushed by nursing. It was tiring but it worked, and my fellow passenger's ever-ready complaints remained unvoiced.*
>
> *Finally landing nine hours later, I breathed a sigh of relief as I gathered up my belongings. My fellow passenger then surprised me with exclamations of amazement. "What an angel! However did you manage to keep him so quiet? It must be all this modern-day equipment that we didn't have when my children were babies!"*

More and more women are discovering how mobile they

can actually be, taking their nursing babies along with them on many outings that bottle feeding mothers would consider impossible. The babies spotted among the guests at weddings, bar mitzvahs, etc., are almost surely the ones who nurse, and "How could you come *without* your baby?" is now heard more often than the opposite.

Even on more formal occasions, many nursing mothers have successfully concluded business deals, fundraising appeals, or interviews accompanied by their nursing babies. When mothers feel comfortable and at ease with nursing, it goes a long way towards changing other people's attitudes towards it. In fact, change is already taking place.

For a variety of reasons, many women today must be involved in spheres of activity other than mothering. In the quest to keep their priorities straight and their consciences clear, so that neither they nor their children are denied their bond of love, these women increasingly find nursing the easiest solution.

In the course of their nursing careers, mothers learn to expect the unexpected. There is just so much foresight one can have. Since it requires nothing more than the mother and child themselves, nursing may be the best precaution she can take for on-the-road emergencies.

> *Late one rainy Saturday night we were driving back from my in-laws. Suddenly our car putted, stalled, and came to an abrupt halt. Nothing my husband did could bring the engine back to life. After four hours of his tampering under the hood, we were finally on our way again.*
>
> *"Thank God a million times over for nursing," I thought. "What would I have done with my baby on this dark, remote highway, miles away from any roadside stop, if he had been bottle fed?"*

Finances: Keeping Costs Down

Another practical advantage of nursing is financial. Compared to the cost of formulas, bottles, heating devices, and all the gas and electricity needed to prepare baby food, breastfeeding is free of charge! Over an extended period, this savings can add up to quite a handsome sum. One mother calculated that the money saved in one year of breastfeeding was equivalent to the price of a clothes drier. She then felt happily justified in going out and buying one!

The Pleasure of Nursing

Nursing offers tactile pleasures as well. As the nursing mother relaxes, caressing her baby, she delights in his smooth, silky skin. While every baby's skin is delicate and pleasant to touch, medical research has verified that the skin of the breastfed child is particularly so.

> *Our visit to my parents overseas was rejuvenating. There I was, a new mother myself, and I kept finding myself lost in memories of my own childhood. During our three-week visit, my mother invited over many of our family friends, and proudly showed them her six-month-old granddaughter. One afternoon, I was delighted to see the renowned Dr. Brisky, now retired, who had been our family pediatrician.*
>
> *"It's not often I have the pleasure of handling a second-generation client," he smiled, fussing over the baby. In no time at all, the two of them were cooing away at each other.*
>
> *"I see she is completely nursed," Dr. Brisky commented.*
>
> *"How did you know?" I inquired curiously.*
>
> *"Oh, just a little professional experience. Breastfed babies feel different, more supple and soft. Also, their fat is distributed more evenly throughout the body. A bottle fed baby*

> *would have more fat here," he pointed, "and here," he explained, as my daughter squealed with delight.*

No Need For Bottles!

An additional boon for nursing mothers pertains to one of those difficult phases of early childhood familiar to some of us. Many bottle fed babies become bottle-addicted toddlers and even bottle-soothed youngsters. Weaning a young child from his familiar companion, the bottle, can become quite an ordeal.

> *Getting rid of the bottle was a difficult task for me as well as for my three bottle fed children. My third child was so attached to her bottle that I used to have daydreams of leading her to the chuppah while she clutched her "life-saver"!*
>
> *I decided to nurse my fourth baby after reading up on the subject and discussing it with friends. One benefit that may seem marginal compared to all the others was the avoidance of the bottle weaning trauma I was so accustomed to. It was so simple: my baby nursed until he decided to stop. He then went straight to a cup and I never introduced a bottle at all.*
>
> *Even though my baby was already a little boy when he gave up nursing, I somehow found his attachment to me rather flattering. In all honesty, thinking back now, I'm convinced I would not have forced weaning on my older, bottle fed children either, had it been me they'd been so attached to.*

The mother of one nursing toddler who had never used a bottle in her life described her daughter's first encounter with the bottle.

A friend of mine came to spend the day, accompanied by her bottle fed baby. My toddler, who had always nursed, was intrigued by the baby's bottle, not knowing quite what it was for. She wandered around the living room with it, stopping suddenly by the house plant. A grin spread across her little face.

Quite matter-of-factly she squirted the milk into the flowerpot. Such a strange device, she had concluded, could only be for watering the plants.

Fitness

After giving birth, mothers find it very important to get back into shape, as the Torah instructs us: "And you should guard your health...."[1] A mother wants to regain her strength, so vital to her mothering career, and her figure, a concern that greatly affects her peace of mind and self-image. Breastfeeding can contribute to both.

Soon after a woman starts to nurse, the calming "mothering hormone," prolactin, is released into her system. This substance serves to promote her recovery from the birth experience. Breastfeeding helps the uterus to contract, thus naturally speeding the body's return to its pre-pregnancy state, and also burns calories. While breastfeeding doesn't *guarantee* weight loss, this "built-in exercise" can quietly curb excessive gaining.

Following her body's natural pattern is the first step a nursing mother takes towards regaining her strength.

Discontinuing the harmonious mother-infant relationship, on the other hand, is not in the mother's best interest. "Not nursing can cause discomfort," explains the Talmud.[2] Indeed, the pain of artificially drying up the flow of breastmilk is not in harmony with a woman's natural bodily functioning.

---

1. *Devarim* 4:15.
2. *Ketubot* 61a.

Preventing Illness

Nursing mothers will be interested to hear that breastfeeding may also serve to prevent breast cancer. Dan H. Moore, Ph.D., American Cancer Society research professor at Hahnemam Medical College and Hospital in Pennsylvania, notes: In populations throughout the world where breastfeeding is practiced most, the incidence of breast cancer is relatively low.[3]

Lactation Amenorea

An additional side effect of breastfeeding relates to the reproductive cycle. A nursing mother's halachic status is likened to that of a woman whose periods are suppressed.[4]

Many women do not menstruate at all while nursing. This is much more common among women who nurse often and exclusively, day and night, i.e., no bottles, no pacifiers, no separations from baby, and no additional foods. Other nursing mothers miss their periods for only a few months. These lapses vary from woman to woman, with a few women even menstruating regularly regardless of exclusive nursing.

The absence of menstruation in the nursing mother is referred to as "lactation amenorea." This condition is conducive to the restoration of her strength after giving birth. The problem of anemia usually does not arise, since her body is not undergoing that monthly blood loss, and she does not experience the fatigue, tension, and mood swings that often precede and accompany menstruation.

Prolactin: the Mothering Hormone

There is yet another Divine gift bestowed upon the nursing mother, one that much increases her peace of mind and

---

3. LLLI, *The Womanly Art,* p. 319.
4. *Shulchan Aruch, Yoreh De'ah* 189:33.

inner tranquility. God designed a woman's body so that the emotional equilibrium she experiences while nursing is reinforced by a certain physiological phenomenon. Scientists have identified a specific hormone, prolactin, which is secreted into the nursing mother's system. Its unique nature has earned it the nickname "the mothering hormone." Like a natural tranquilizer, it calms the mother. Promoting patience and tolerance, prolactin is conducive to tender, loving mothering. The baby and his siblings can all benefit from the effects this substance has on their mother.

Self-Esteem

"More than the calf wants to suck, the mother cow wants to suckle."[5] This is true of human beings as well. Nursing enhances a woman's self-esteem and imbues her with a great sense of fulfillment, for she recognizes her indispensable contribution to the development of the child God has entrusted to her. Many professions and careers can be pursued by a variety of people; many roles are filled by employees who can be easily replaced. But there is no substitute for the nursing mother. Nursing one's own child is a unique act of love.

Spiritual Fulfillment

In reference to Chanah, mother of Shmuel, Scripture states: "And the woman *sat* and breastfed her son...."[6] Those words communicate a sense of peacefulness that hints at Chanah's maternal commitment. Just as going on pilgrimages to the Temple had once expressed her devotion to the Almighty, she could now best serve God by devoting herself to the gift He had bestowed upon her. We mothers of today can follow

---

5. *Pesachim* 112a.
6. *I Shmuel* 1:23.

her example. We, too, can reach our spiritual goals by nurturing our own children, for our awareness of God's wisdom and kindness is thereby enhanced.

> *I get a tremendous spiritual uplift from nursing. Here is this tiny, helpless newborn who will develop, God willing, into a robust, active, curious child, nourished solely by my breastmilk. It seems nothing short of a miracle, and strengthens my trust and belief in the Creator.*

Developing Responsibility

Aside from spiritual growth, one woman maintains that her attainment of personal maturity was accelerated by her nursing experience:

> *As incredible as it may sound to all those career women who gave up nursing because it interfered with their jobs, nursing actually benefitted my own.*
>
> *I was a career woman who "stopped the world" to nurse my babies. Then, after a fulfilling mothering career, I returned to the job market. I knew I was up against younger, "unattached" applicants, more recently trained than I. Yet I was confident. The "loving by giving" attitude I had developed as a mother worked in my favor now. All that motherly foresight and concern for details was, they told me later, very much in evidence. The determination and commitment that had become my lifestyle shined through in the devoted, trustworthy, and eager applicant who appeared at that interview. I got the job!*

One mother tells how nursing enabled her to enter a job slot she hadn't ever applied for!

I am a great supporter of nursing, pointing out its benefits at every opportunity. Yet on one occasion, my nursing practice came in handy in a totally unexpected manner.

When my eight-year-old daughter had to have stitches in her hand, the doctor showed a nurse how he wanted her to hold my daughter's hand firmly in place.

"Please," pleaded my little girl, "can't my mother hold my hand?"

Sympathetically yet sternly, the doctor replied, "Sorry, honey. It's very important that your hand be very still. Your mother can stand nearby at the foot of the bed."

"Oh, please! I promise to keep still. I just want my mother to hold my hand."

"Not right now. It's really a nurse's job. She knows just what I need her to do."

My daughter's eyes lit up, "But my mommy can do it! She's a nurse! She nurses our baby all the time!"

The doctor burst into laughter. He did not argue with my daughter any further, and it was I who performed the nurse's job.

Chapter Five
Getting Off to a Good Start

"There's the hospital where you were born," my mother would always say whenever we passed the large, brown complex of buildings. I must have heard those words hundreds of times.

When I gave birth to my first child I finally understood my mother's almost instinctive reaction to the hospital site. For it was there, in a small, intimate room of the same huge building, that I made my first acquaintance with my own newborn. That is where our mother-child relationship began and that is where she first clutched at me with her tiny, trusting fingers.

Contact With Your Newborn

Those first few days after birth have a significant impact not only upon mother-newborn bonding, but also upon the course of their future mother-child relationship. This holds true whether the delivery takes place at home or in the hospital, and no matter how long the hospital stay.

Many studies have documented the importance of mother-infant contact immediately following birth. In one study conducted by Drs. John Kennell and Marshall Klaus, professors of pediatrics at Case Western Reserve University School of Medicine, one group of fourteen mothers enjoyed an uninterrupted hour with their babies directly after birth, and five hours a day together during the next three days of their hospital stay. In a second group, the mothers and babies experienced the usual hospital routine: a glimpse of the baby at birth, brief contact six to eight hours later, and then twenty- to thirty-minute feedings every four hours. The mothers were selected at random for each group and were matched for socioeconomic status.

One month later, and then one year later, the researchers studied the mothers' responses to their babies. Though no two groups of mothers and babies are alike, the contrasts in this case were unusually pronounced.

The mothers in the first group caressed their babies more often and shared greater eye contact with them. When their babies were upset, these women picked them up and comforted them more readily. Their breastfeeding was initiated more easily and continued longer.

Even at two years of age, differences were noted in the way the mothers spoke to their toddlers. The mothers in the first group used a wider vocabulary, asked their children more questions, and used less commands than the mothers in the second group.[1]

Though one should not underestimate the importance of early mother-infant contact, let no reader become overly worried by this research. If it's impossible for her to be with her infant right after birth, it is completely within her capacity to make up for the loss!

Hospital policies are relatively recent inventions, but a mother's urge to handle her newborn has most likely existed

---

1. Marshall H. Klaus and John H. Kennel, *Maternal-Infant Bonding: the Impact of Early Separation or Loss on Family Development* (St. Louis: The C.V. Mosby Company, 1976), pp. 53-62.

since Creation. It is simply the natural beginning of the lifelong mother-child relationship. Thus, despite the modern hospital routine of whisking the baby away from his mother soon after birth, more and more mothers are asking for some time with their newborns. This interlude is a precious opportunity vital to the earliest act of mothering: breastfeeding.

Though nursing comes naturally, it doesn't necessarily come *automatically*. It is important to get off to a good start, and immediately after birth is the best time to begin, for it is then that the baby's sucking reflex is strongest. He has been nourished in his mother's womb for nine long months, and will delight in the natural continuation of this relationship. He will seek contact and satisfaction, and will be soothed and calmed after his abrupt change of environment and the tremendous stress of birth.

Even the most timid and inhibited of new mothers, who has likewise emerged from the overwhelming experience of labor, will be encouraged by a baby who latches on to her breast only minutes after birth.

> *It was such a boost to my confidence, or lack thereof! I hadn't the faintest idea about nursing, having thought mainly about the birth for nine impatient months. Actually, I felt quite apprehensive. No one in my immediate family had ever nursed; I wondered if I would be able to. Would I have enough milk? When my little newborn "went right to it," sucking away as if he'd been doing it for years, I was amazed and delighted.*
>
> *As time went on, I discovered that he wouldn't always latch on immediately. Some days he fussed more than others and my lack of confidence might have overwhelmed me were it not for those first few minutes that he had nursed right at the outset. "If he could do it then, he can do it now," I'd say to myself patiently on those difficult days. That initial*

experience really made the difference. I might have given up if not for that constant reminder that it was possible.

Positioning Your Baby

How does one get off to a good start?

Depending on your position during birth, whether lying or sitting, bring the baby close to you, hold him in your arms or lay him down next to you. Many women are uncomfortable changing positions right after birth, but as far as the baby is concerned, he'll adapt quite easily as long as he's close to you.

You may feel shy or even clumsy attempting to steer the breast towards your baby. This is a new and different experience, and it is quite natural to feel a bit awkward. The baby, however, is totally uninhibited. He will probably latch on at once, since sucking is an inborn reflex. Some babies however, demonstrate only minimal interest. Don't worry. Your newborn will catch on sooner or later. Hold him close and try again from time to time.

Afterpains

Aside from a mother's desire to get nursing off to a good start, she will be pleased to discover that breast stimulation helps the uterus contract. (It also hastens the expulsion of the placenta.) These contractions, called afterpains, prevent excessive blood loss and are of vital importance to her well-being.

Drugs During Labor

As for drugs, excessive doses of pain relievers during labor (especially drugs like pethidine) are probably responsible for more breastfeeding failure than people have realized.[2] A drowsy

---

2. Stanway, *Breast is Best*, p. 83.

mother is less capable of establishing close contact and attachment with her newborn after birth, and a drowsy baby has more difficulty sucking.

It is hardly surprising that a mother who has taken drugs may become dispirited and discontinue nursing. She missed out on that initial boost of confidence, and she now has a difficult feeder as well. It is thus most advisable, from a nursing perspective (as well as for other reasons), to avoid excessive medication during labor.

Yet as much as we would like a drug-free labor, it is not always an option. We can, however, prepare ourselves as well as possible for the birth experience, thereby rendering the need for drugs less likely.

The Uninterested Baby

Whenever a baby shows a lack of interest in nursing, gently express a drop of milk into his mouth. Its sweet taste will encourage him to suck for more. Many mothers practice this simple, efficient method, and our Sages even discuss it in the Talmud.[3] The *Shulchan Aruch* rules that it is permissible on Shabbat, even though squeezing is generally forbidden.[4]

Hospital Routine

Whatever your newborn's response to the breast, this early interaction is as delightful as it is beneficial. Unfortunately, not all mothers are given this opportunity.

> *I had read about the importance of a mother's bonding with her newborn, and wholeheartedly agreed with it in theory. When my first baby was born, however, I was not even*

---

3. *Shabbat* 144b.
4. *Orach Chaim* 328:35.

thinking about the far-reaching effects, benefits, etc. I was simply overwhelmed by the fact that I had just given birth to a beautiful little boy, and all I wanted to do was hold him close to me. After all, I had carried him within me for nine long months, and was not prepared to part with him so abruptly!

But the staff in the delivery room did not seem to understand my intense feelings. They were concerned with the efficient performance of their jobs and with filling out his birth-record form. I protested that his measurements were at that moment of no importance to me, and that all I wanted was some private time with my son, but to no avail. He was finally "shown" to me, washed, cleaned, and wrapped so tightly that I couldn't even make out the shape of his little body. Five minutes later, he was wheeled away in a bassinet!

As disappointed as I felt, I resolved not to argue any further. Head-on confrontation with rigid routines is something I learned to avoid during my secretarial days in a government office. I knew that the sheer physical effort and tension involved would only deplete my strength, and decided that my energy would be better spent on my little boy, when we would finally be together again.

We salute this mother's patience and levelheadedness. Although we stress the importance of early interaction, we do not suggest that a new mother expend all her energies "fighting city hall." If despite your efforts the hospital staff is uncooperative, save your energy and do the best you can under the circumstances.

On the other hand, it is sensible to investigate hospital practices *before* you register for birth. If possible, choose the hospital that best suits your needs. Sometimes, a letter from the head of the department is the best insurance that your wishes will be respected. One mother obtained in advance the following note from the head of the department: "Mrs. Cohen's baby is to remain by her side day and night from birth."

Medical Complications

Medical complications can sometimes delay the onset of nursing immediately after birth.

> *I've always enjoyed nursing my children. For me, holding a newborn in my arms and nursing him for the first time is a thrilling experience. With my last baby, however, it was a very special thrill indeed.*
>
> *After an unavoidable cesarean birth, I waited patiently to see my baby and nurse him.*
>
> *"He is having respiratory problems and must stay in the intensive-care unit," I was told. "He can't nurse yet anyway."*
>
> *Even as I prayed for his full recovery, I resolved that my child would have the best I could give him—my own breastmilk—and I regularly expressed milk to keep up my supply. Thank God, the baby improved, and a week later he was taken off the I.V. Still, he could only be bottle fed tiny, carefully monitored amounts of breastmilk.*
>
> *Finally, fifteen days after his birth, the doctor uttered the words I was longing to hear: "You can try nursing him today."*
>
> *I will never forget the relief and pleasure I experienced that morning. Taking this tiny baby in my arms, I nestled him against me, right where he naturally belonged. Tenderly yet apprehensively, I offered him the breast, prepared for anything—disinterest, inability to suckle, even confusion and crying.*
>
> *My baby latched on at once and, to my astonishment and*

joy, set in nursing enthusiastically. After a few minutes of intense nursing, he opened his eyes and gazed at me. The look in his eyes seemed to say: "Don't you know I've been waiting for this just as much as you have?"

The First Days of Nursing

From the delivery room, the mother is transferred to the recovery unit for a short observation period, and then into the general ward. Once settled, you will probably wonder what it will be like being the mother of this child and you'll be waiting eagerly to see him again. If this is your first child, you'll have many questions about his proper care.

I had come to visit a friend who had just given birth and we were chatting away in her hospital room. In the same room were two other women—one middle-aged, the other younger—who were intently discussing their birth experiences. I could not help overhearing part of their conversation when I suddenly recognized one of them as a woman from my neighborhood.

"Mazel tov!" I extended my hand to the older of the two. "What did you have?"

"Thank you. I had a boy. Actually, I'm entitled to two mazel tovs," she winked. "This is my daughter. She has just given birth to a girl!"

The younger woman smiled. "This is my first. It's such a special feeling! Can you imagine how wonderful it is to be here with my mother? She's telling me everything I need to know, especially about nursing, and has really helped me get off to a good start."

Not all of us are as lucky as this young mother, who had her own experienced mother right alongside her in the hospital for guidance. We would like to mother *you*, too, a little bit, by anticipating some of your questions about nursing your newborn.

You ask yourself, how often should I nurse? How long? How much? These are questions you did not have to consider before. Nevertheless, just as the embryo was totally dependent upon you, it is *you*, the mother, who should make these decisions. Feel capable, feel confident, and trust God, Who has granted you, along with the gift of motherhood, the wisdom and insight to give your child what he needs.

First of all, *nurse frequently*.

The breasts are not full of milk immediately after birth. Their supply builds up as the baby stimulates them. It will be a relief and delight to both you and your baby to feel the milk come in after three or four days. Don't worry if it takes longer. Afterwards, to ensure a steady supply, the breasts must be emptied often. Infrequent nursing will diminish the supply.

When we tell you to nurse frequently, we don't mean that your infant will necessarily want to be put to the breast all day! Babies enjoy being comforted by rocking, handling, caressing, and singing. Our ancestor Miriam was also known as Puah the midwife because she calmed the newborns of the Jews in Egypt, talking and humming to them gently and soothingly.[5] You needn't feel shy about doing the same.

The fundamental principle of successful breastfeeding is to nurse *on demand*, rather than *on schedule*. We shall take the liberty of calling this method by a different name entirely, as did one nursing mother:

> *I don't like that term "demand" feeding. I can hardly compare that huge mound of laundry, "demanding" to be washed, to my little baby, who they say "demands" my attention. I*

5. Rashi, *Shemot* 1:15.

view it rather as "responsive nursing." When he calls—I respond.

Colostrum

Many new mothers are taken aback by the initial absence of milk.

> *I come from a family where nursing was taken for granted. I grew up with memories of my mother, aunts, and older sisters all breastfeeding babies whose loud sucking sounds made me giggle. I imagined that I would be automatically overflowing with milk right after giving birth.*
>
> *Imagine my horror when I put my tiny newborn to a soft, empty breast, which only sparingly leaked a strange, yellowish fluid.*
>
> *"Don't bother nursing him yet," my roommate told me with great self-assurance. "Your milk hasn't come in yet. That yellow stuff is nothing; just ignore it and give him a bottle in the meantime. You don't want him to be hungry while he's waiting for your milk."*

Nothing could be further from the truth! A new mother should definitely "bother," for it is precisely the baby's sucking soon after birth that brings on the milk. Furthermore, that "strange, yellowish fluid," known as colostrum, is a nutritional treasure chest, not a "mistake of nature" soon corrected and replaced by "real" breastmilk. Colostrum is the Divinely formulated nourishment most fitting and beneficial for a newborn.

The composition of colostrum meets the baby's needs in a most remarkable way. During his first few months of life, he is unable to manufacture antibodies against infection. He is totally dependent upon the immunity he received in the womb and that he now receives from his mother's milk. Colostrum has such amazing immunological properties that Dr. Herbert Ratner called it "nature's vaccine."[6] Its high concentration of anti-infection factors provides the newborn with maximum protection when he needs it most.

Colostrum is rich in protein, minerals, and vitamins—vital nutrients for the newborn. Its lower concentration of fats and sugars is perfectly adequate for his needs, since it doesn't overburden his tiny body with nutrients that require a more developed digestive system.

Rooming In

The rigid hospital feeding schedule can hardly accommodate responsive nursing. The scheduling that is so appropriate to hospital routine does not necessarily meet the needs of mother and child.

One way to avoid this problem is to "room in." This option allows a baby to stay with his mother, giving her the opportunity to get to know and comfort him while attending to his physical needs. These needs are actually few, and they don't demand much time and energy: changing a diaper is a simple procedure, and keeping him clean can be accomplished excellently with a wet cloth. In fact, many doctors advise against extensive bathing of a newborn, because the coat of vernix with which he is born is a "natural moisturizer" that protects his delicate skin. It is by no means merely an unattractive, oily substance to be washed off. Rather, it is of great benefit, and should remain with him until it is absorbed by the skin. There is no rush to bathe him after delivery. Ideally, it should be postponed a few days until the mother feels strong enough to do it herself, for it is a lovely experience to give your baby his very first bath.

---

6. LLLI, *The Womanly Art,* p. 294.

Thus, a newborn's needs can be adequately met by his mother in a rooming in set up: she can nurse him whenever he wants, avoid schedules, and not have to worry about that extra bottle so often given a crying baby in the nursery.

That "harmless" extra bottle, given him "because we didn't want to wake you," can adversely affect the baby and his nursing in many ways.

* As mentioned in chapter three, an allergic reaction to even a small amount of cow's milk can surface weeks or months after the bottle is given.

* It is easier for a baby to drink from a bottle. Once exposed to it, he may be reluctant to do the harder work that nursing requires of him.

* The artificial sugar in formula can "wean" him away from naturally sweetened breastmilk.

* The baby may develop "nipple confusion" when switched from breast to bottle. This often results in nursing failure, as the two modes of sucking are totally dissimilar.

A baby whose mother has chosen a rooming in arrangement is spared the anxiety that accompanies mother-infant separation in the hospital. She can nurse her baby frequently and for as long as she desires, unrushed by the omnipresent schedule. She can relax and start creating a loving bond with her little one. She will do well to alternate sides, balancing the amount of milk in each breast. (One trick a mother can use to remember which side to start nursing on next time is to stick a safety pin in her nightgown.)

A mother rooming in will not have to end a feeding abruptly in order to keep up with all the other ladies who have finished nursing and who are already wheeling their babies back to the nursery. (If she ever needs to end a feeding, she can put her little finger in the corner of his mouth and gently enlarge the opening, thereby breaking her infant's suction.)

Burping the baby

This undisturbed feeding will end with the mother burping the baby calmly, without having the nursery staff urging her to hurry. She can hold the infant in an upright position, supporting his head and torso. She can lean him on her shoulder or lay him on his stomach. Not all babies need to expel air after every feeding. Many breastfed infants do so spontaneously. A mother need not worry about this: since his bassinet is close by, she will hear any sounds of discomfort that may signal a need to expel air, sometimes a while after the feeding. But imagine if the baby is full, does not expel air directly afterwards, and then, back in the nursery, has to wail for twenty minutes until a nurse can burp him. Or perhaps a well-meaning nurse thinks that he hasn't had enough to eat, and proceeds to give him a bottle. Obviously, this will only aggravate his discomfort. We cannot expect the attendant in the nursery to consult each mother before tending to a crying baby.

Rooming in can help avoid all these eventualities.

The question of "rest"

One of the most common arguments against rooming in, and for not consulting or bothering the mother concerning her baby, is the compassionate claim that "she has just given birth and needs the rest."

True, new mothers should rest following delivery. But is this achieved by "protecting" them from their newborns? It's a rare woman, in any case, who can look back upon her hospital stay as restful and rejuvenating, because hospital routine is hardly conducive to long hours of sleep. Separating the mother from her baby is an unnatural, unreliable way to help her relax. And there's a subtle message behind it: the precious child who has just arrived in this world is already a nuisance and a bother. One frustrated mother reports:

> *I'd just as soon be woken at night to nurse than to have my "vital signs" checked! My baby was given a bottle, despite my specific requests, because the nurse did not want to wake me. But I had been awake anyway, tossing and turning in bed for an hour after my sleep had been disturbed at some unearthly hour for a routine check of my blood pressure.*

After birth, many women experience an extra flow of adrenaline due to the increase in their hormones.

> *I can't sleep well in the hospital. I would just as soon use all that excess energy for my new baby. Besides, I'm going to have to wake up every night from now on, so I might as well get used to it right from the beginning.*

These mothers are already looking upon motherhood in a different light. Rather than nervously "storing up" sleep in order to "face up to the ordeal" at home, they adopt the attitude that they *can* do it, and that now is the time to start. By the time they get home, the mother-infant relationship is well established.

Although home is the most natural place to be immediately after giving birth, this is not usually a realistic option nowadays. Nevertheless, rooming in creates a little world of its own, undisturbed by the ongoing everyday life outside. The hospital can provide the security a new mother craves, for the staff attends to her physical needs and relieves her of household demands, while she receives emotional support from the other mothers who have just given birth along with her. In short, the hospital can serve as a peaceful, temporary haven.

Chapter Six
Welcome Home

I was coming home from the hospital with the new baby, our fifth child. Though weary and weak, I was excited and happy to be back. "I'll probably be greeted by the colorful 'Welcome Home' signs and drawings on the front door," I thought in anticipation, realizing how much I missed my family. My older children had always made pictures when a new baby was born.

Strangely enough, the front door was bare. "My husband must have had his hands full and didn't get around to putting up the pictures," I thought. As I walked through the house I noticed that the doors to the kitchen, dining room and den were shut. But when I went to our bedroom to put down the baby, I discovered the entire door "wallpapered" with my children's drawings.

"I decided to put the 'Welcome Home' signs only on the door to the room where you're going to rest and recuperate," my husband later explained. "I don't want you to even peek at the rest of the house. We managed while you were gone and we'll continue to do so till you regain your strength. That's my insurance policy for getting a healthy mommy back more quickly."

The sensitive attitude displayed by this woman's husband is worth all the advice that's usually given to new mothers. Taking care of the mother, and seeing she gets proper nutrition and sufficient rest, is the best service anyone can do her.

How can mother and infant establish their nursing relationship while she's getting back into household and family routines? Before detailing the various issues she will now confront about mothering her baby in the midst of many other responsibilities, our first concern is the mother herself. Regaining her strength is essential to successful mothering. Accordingly, a new mother's greatest need is to be "mothered" herself.

> *While awaiting the birth of our sixth child, I wondered how I would ever manage. Then, two days after he was born, I discovered the most humane, generous, devoted women's organization I have ever encountered.*
>
> *Appropriately called "Shifra and Puah," this non-profit group contacted me in the hospital. After wishing me "mazel tov," its representatives explained: "We are a woman-to-woman organization dedicated to making the birth of a Jewish child the joyous, rewarding experience it really is. You live in our neighborhood and that's why we're here."*
>
> *What followed was way beyond my imagination. Upon returning home, I found a lovely crib, a clean carriage, and three packages of disposable diapers. Even more important: for two weeks, hot meals were delivered for the whole family, a cleaning lady arrived three times a week, and a dependable babysitter was available to take out the little ones every afternoon.*
>
> *This wonderful service allowed me plenty of rest, in my own home, surrounded by my family. Being home enhanced my peace of mind, which in turn hastened my recovery and*

enabled me to take on my household responsibilities sooner and more energetically.

Organizations like "Shifra and Puah," named after the Jewish midwives of ancient Egypt, reflect the Torah's attitude towards motherhood. Judaism has always looked upon the miracle of birth as a Divine gift, but the recipient of this gift—the mother—cannot necessarily manage everything without assistance. She has special needs and we must accommodate her.

Rest and Nutrition

Following birth, and throughout her nursing period, our Sages stress the necessity of adequate rest and nutrition. "A nursing mother should not be overworked and her diet should be enriched."[1] This issue is considered so vital to her well-being that the Talmud discusses which particular foods are beneficial to nursing.[2] In addition, the Rambam states that the cravings which normally accompany pregnancy are common in the nursing period as well.[3]

The following are some important tips for good nutrition:

* Avoid products containing caffeine—cola, coffee, tea, and chocolate—and avoid products containing alcohol.
* You need thirty to fifty percent more calories than before your pregnancy, about 3,000 calories daily.
* Eat a variety of wholesome foods, including fresh fruits, vegetables, and whole grains.
* Try to keep food as close as possible to its natural state.
* Avoid processed foods, especially those containing refined sugar.

---

1. *Ketubot* 65b.
2. ibid. 60b.
3. *Hilchot Ishut* 21:11.

* It is a good idea to take a multivitamin preparation.

* Make certain you get enough vitamin C. Otherwise, take in tablet form.

* Avoid strict reducing diets while nursing. It's better to stick to the basic foods but cut down on portion size and, obviously, junk foods.

* Make certain to drink enough liquids.

Setting Priorities

Upon the arrival of the new baby, the parents must reorient themselves and rearrange their priorities. Though the habits of every household are unique, one basic rule applies to all situations: *People before things!* The first person in line, of course, has to be the mother, for the entire family depends on her.

Once the immediate physical and emotional needs of the family are met, most mothers find conversation with relatives and friends enjoyable and stimulating. People need people, and a new mother enjoys sharing her birth experiences, whether it's her first or her ninth. Pleasant as they are, though, telephone calls and visitors may nonetheless drain her energy and a new mother need never hesitate to excuse herself. People understand.

Housework

Next on your list of priorities, after all the "people" have been taken care of, come the "things." The most pressing "thing" constantly staring you right in the face is, of course, housework. Before you tackle any of it, acknowledge the fact that now is the time to lower your standards. You'll be surprised to discover that you can keep a relatively neat and orderly house even by forgoing half your regular chores. Even on those days when the basics don't get done, relax, don't panic. After all, unmade beds, toys strewn on the floor, and piles of laundry waiting to be put away, are *signs of life*. Remember, you have just brought home another little living being! Anyone can do housework, but only you can mother your baby.

Coping with housework does not necessarily mean doing it yourself. Take advantage of any help that's offered, or, if possible, hire some. Don't forget, though, that the help is there so you can rest, tend to your baby, or take care of your other children. You might be tempted to do so, but *please* don't have the cleaning lady rock the crying baby while you scrub the floor. You may indeed be able to do the job better yourself, but the baby needs *your* attention, *your* relaxed disposition, *your* energy to provide him with the care only a mother can give, while the floor will do just fine being washed by a stranger.

Realize your limitations and don't overdo things. From a halachic perspective, a woman is considered a *yoledet* (one who has given birth) for a month after delivery, and a full-fledged invalid for the first week.[4] Consequently, she is relieved of various rabbinic prohibitions and obligations. These halachic rulings are clearly in harmony with the *yoledet*'s need to regain her strength.

Many women may feel the strain for more than a month. Be sensitive to your needs and gauge yourself accordingly. For a new mother, carefully looking after herself is not a selfish act of indulgence! She is actually doing her family a service, one that is especially crucial to the tiny baby who is totally dependent upon her. It is no great act of heroism to be out pushing a wagon in the supermarket the day after the Brit Milah. Have mercy on your baby—and yourself: find a shop where you can telephone in an order and have it delivered, or ask someone else to shop for you.

---

4. *Shulchan Aruch, Orach Chaim* 330:1.

Even after the initial recuperation period, a woman must make a conscious effort to conserve her energy. This will enable her to enjoy the extended, satisfying nursing experience of mothering that she deserves.

> *Enjoyable as nursing is for both baby and me, at the beginning I was always tired. I wouldn't even consider giving it up, of course, so I sought advice from a competent breastfeeding counselor. She suggested two basic energy-conserving rules, which I have stuck to ever since.*
>
> *First: keep baby nearby. Depending on what I'm doing, he is near me either rocking in a baby swing, playing in the playpen, or strapped onto me in a baby carrier. The security of being next to Mommy calms him down. He cries less frequently and demands less attention. I don't have to run upstairs or to the back of the house to tend to him. I realized it wasn't the frequent nursing that was draining me, but everything I was doing in between.*
>
> *Second: sleep when baby sleeps. I was always tempted to do housework when the baby slept. The peace and quiet seemed to trigger an immediate dash for the broom or the laundry hamper. It took me a while to realize that this was a mistake, and I finally got the message from the baby himself. Once, as I collapsed into a chair to nurse him, numb with fatigue from cleaning, he looked up at me and his big, brown eyes seemed to plead: "Please, Mommy, save your energy for me, not for the kitchen floor!"*

Responsive Nursing

Once a new mother has recuperated, she is anxious to get back into some kind of routine. Don't make the mistake of trying to fit the baby into your schedule. He'll never comply happily! You'll be much more relaxed and productive, and your baby will be far better off, if you simply *discard* your schedule for the time being. *You* must adjust to *him,* not the other way around!

Sooner or later most babies develop a pattern of their own that suits their needs. Until then, avoid the anxiety of: "Will I get the laundry done before he wakes up?" or: "If he would only sleep five more minutes!" or: "But he isn't due to nurse for another half-hour!"

These frustrating thoughts aren't taken too seriously by a nursing mother who has discovered that responsive nursing is the most practical way to care for an infant and a household at the same time. That common question, "How often should I nurse my baby?" does not besiege her with doubts. She responds to her baby's call by either nursing, changing, soothing, rocking, or just simply holding him, and she's prepared to nurse him once again if that's the only way to calm him down, even if he has just finished a feeding.

Our Sages speak favorably of responsive nursing: *"A baby should be allowed to nurse as often as he desires. Even if he nurses all day long, it will not harm him."*[5] They compare it to the way the Jews ate manna all day without any ill effects. Elsewhere, it is stated that "a Jew should be involved in Torah study every hour of the day, just as a baby nurses every hour of the day."[6]

Night Feeding

"Every hour of the day" includes night feedings as well. A mother who wonders if her baby is the only one who gets up at unheard of hours to nurse might be encouraged to know that the Talmud refers to those pre-dawn hours as prime nursing time.[7]

---

5. *Tosefta Sotah* 4:1.
6. Jerusalem Talmud, *Brachot* 68a.
7. *Brachot* 3a.

Night feedings are an intrinsic aspect of mothering. A baby who sleeps through the night is not in any way a better baby. Every child is an individual and the mother of a nighttime feeder would do well not to compare her baby to all those sleepy angels down the block. Rather, we can heed the advice of Shlomoh HaMelech, known as the wisest of all men: "Educate a child according to his way...,"[8] i.e., in harmony with his natural tendencies. In fact, in the long run, the nighttime nurser is doing his mom a favor: he is stimulating milk production and preventing the breast engorgement that ultimately reduces it.

Despite the aggravation of interrupted sleep, night nursing disturbs the rest of the family only minimally. The baby is near his mother, and both he and she drift quickly off to sleep again. This is certainly a far cry from getting up, heating bottles, and searching for pacifiers, which usually awakens the entire household, if everyone hasn't been roused already by the baby's wailing. Appreciating the benefits helps us put up with those nighttime feedings. One mother relates her feelings:

> *Many of our nighttime nursing sessions have gone by while I was half-asleep. Still, there are times when I actually look forward to the stirring of that tiny bundle lying in the bassinet next to my bed. It is a special moment. All is quiet, and only the baby and I are awake to appreciate this gift of closeness we share.*
>
> *Those still, peaceful moments reawaken feelings of immense gratitude to God. I thank Him wholeheartedly for this Divine gift. Just as I have been granted this joy by virtue of the sheer goodness of Hashem, I am inspired to shower kindness on my child.*

---

8. *Mishlei* 22:6.

Another mother tells us how she copes with night-nursing:

> *As the rain was beating against the blinds I cuddled up against my ten-month-old tucked next to me in bed. She had never yet "slept through the night," but she was my seventh child and I was used to night feedings by now. In fact, I never had to "get up" for them, and it was my husband whom I had to thank for the extra sleep I was getting. It was his idea, way back with our first child, as he saw me struggle out of bed for the third time one night: "Keep him next to you," he suggested, "and, by the way," he added unexpectedly, "thank you for taking care of him so patiently."*
>
> *Since that day I stopped worrying about "getting them used to your bed," "they'll never be independent," and other such rumors. What I did do, was invest in sleeping arrangements that were both safe and comfortable for us all.*
>
> *None of my children has ever felt jealous towards the one in my room, as they all had their chance, and strangely enough they all left my room for their own with no persuasion from me. Quite the contrary, my last child said when she left my room, "Don't worry, Mommy, Hashem will give you another baby to have near you." Baruch Hashem she was right.*

The Let-Down Reflex

A mother's response to her infant is often accompanied by a strong physical reaction. This phenomenon, known as the "let-down reflex," never ceases to amaze many nursing mothers. God created us in such extraordinary harmony with our babies' needs that the mammary glands often announce that the infant is hungry even before he himself has begun to cry!

This "announcement" is a gentle tingling in the breasts, usually followed by a flow of milk "let down" from the mammary glands. This reflex is so sensitive that mothers have found themselves "leaking" at the mere thought of their nursing infants.

If necessary, one can wear nursing pads, which prevent telltale stains. However, one must choose a brand that allows for air circulation, and avoid plastic-covered pads, which can be harmful. Do not become overly concerned by leakage. By gently applying pressure to the breasts in a upward motion, it can be suspended. Soon enough, the mammary glands accommodate their production to the baby's requirements.

The Milk Supply

The breasts, too, will adapt to baby's needs. A woman may find her breast size decreasing, once her nursing becomes steadier and more established. She must not then mistakenly conclude that her milk supply is diminishing. Quite the contrary: it is balancing itself out, and is now more efficiently stored in the upper ducts so as not to engorge the breasts. One cannot help but marvel at all these physical adjustments Divinely designed to accommodate both mother and child.

Weight Gain

Probably of more concern to a mother than her own physical development is that of her baby. Watching her baby grow is a source of continuous encouragement. (The constant need to buy larger-size baby clothing is one expense parents do not complain about!) Nonetheless, there is hardly a mother who does not ask herself from time to time: "Is he really getting enough? Is the breastmilk adequate? Shouldn't his body be a bit more padded?"

Baby's weight gain, or lack thereof, often causes mother extreme anxiety. Baby scales stare at her every time she enters the pediatrician's office, and the curved lines of the weight charts wag at her like accusing fingers. And if she chances to see a graduated baby bottle, can she help but wonder whether her little one is getting as much?

While we by no means suggest that a nursing mother disregard her baby's weight gain, our perspective is simple yet clear: 1) Weight gain in itself is no guarantee of health; one baby might gain 7 ounces (about 200 grams) a week while another might only gain 4 ounces (about 100 grams) a week, yet they could both be thriving equally well. 2) Nursing babies often gain more slowly. In general, the weight-gain charts were geared to bottle fed babies, who usually gain faster. 3) "Failure" to meet weight chart requirements does not necessarily mean that a baby's growth is inadequate. Remember that babies normally lose weight after birth, and some take even a number of weeks to return to their birth weight!

A nursing mother should feel confident that she is doing the very best for her baby, nourishing him in accordance with the Divine plan. She should not be afraid to use her own instincts, experience, and common sense. No one is better informed about the baby than his own mother.

"Your baby's weight is below average. You milk is insufficient. Start supplementing with formula." A nursing mother who has heard these words knows the sense of failure that follows. Whenever any doubts arise concerning the baby's weight gain, a doctor who is an expert in breastfeeding should be consulted. For questions on nursing, refer to a breastfeeding counselor, a La Leche leader, or a lactation consultant.

While a mother who bottle feeds her baby has those small numbers on the bottle to indicate how much he has drunk, the nursing mother is not granted this "privilege." Obviously, she does not need it. While a bottle feeding mother might legitimately become concerned if a pediatrician deems her baby's intake insufficient, a nursing mother need not feel inadequate. She should simply seek expert advice.

"They told me to stop nursing my three-month-old and start formula," I told the patient breastfeeding counselor whom I had contacted upon my return from a highly disturbing visit to the clinic, "but I firmly believe breastmilk is the best thing for my baby. They don't know (and didn't have time to ask) that all my children were slow gainers, that my husband is very skinny, that my baby hasn't eaten well this week because of a stuffy nose. Anyway, the weight charts were probably calibrated in accordance with the average bottle fed baby. In spite of what they said, I can see myself that my baby is progressing nicely."

The breastfeeding counselor suggested I look for another pediatrician with more expertise in breastfeeding, and eventually I found a doctor who was pro-breastfeeding not only in theory, but in practice. Though he recorded each weight gain, he was by no means in awe of the charts. And other factors, such as head circumference and family body structure, were taken into consideration as well. He suggested I follow the breastfeeding counselor's advice. With renewed confidence I continued nursing.

My daughter gained weight at her own pace, though even now, at the age of four, she's on the skinny side. But she's perfectly healthy, thank God, and now, no one can blame my milk!

Another mother, who used to be nervous all the time for the opposite reason, reminisces:

It finally occurred to me one day that bottle feeding hadn't always been around. God's plan did not include a built-in device to monitor a nursing baby's intake. So if God Himself was relying on me to regulate my baby's feeding, I realized that I must be qualified to do so. I vowed not to pay any further attention to comments about my baby's plumpness and the need to put him on a diet. It took me a while to relax and enjoy my plump little son. "There's no such thing as too much breastmilk," I kept telling myself. "As long as I'm nursing exclusively, whatever he gets from me is fine."

Nowadays, when I'm accused of overfeeding him, I laughingly retort that my little one-and-a-half-year-old must be getting up at midnight to raid the refrigerator.

Solids

Most medical authorities agree that breastmilk alone meets all of an infant's nutritional needs, and up to the age of *at least* six months a mother need not be concerned about adding solids. Even after the age of six months, if the baby is doing well there is no obligation to add solids. The time to begin thinking about introducing your baby to table foods is when the baby himself starts showing real interest in them.[9]

One mother of an exclusively nursing older baby relates the following episode:

I was feeling rather nervous. My one-year-old baby was being examined by the clinic's doctor when the inevitable question came up. "What does she eat now?"

I shifted anxiously in my chair. "I'm still nursing her."

"Yes, I understand—but what does she eat?" he emphasized.

"Breastmilk," I replied. "I am still completely nursing my baby. Is there a problem with her weight gain?" I knew there were no problems. But I felt uneasy.

"Do you mean to say that this baby doesn't eat any food?" He glared unbelievingly. "Yes," I answered. He then called three nurses into the room. "Do you see this woman? She is still totally nursing her baby. You may think her

9. LLLI, *The Womanly Art,* p. 160.

child will grow up with a marked eating problem..." The doctor then broke out into a wide grin. "But I can tell you, this child will eat properly—all in good time. This mother is the type I wish I met more often!"

Now when I see my child at five years old I can only say that he was quite right!

Pacifiers

One thing that some mothers *are* prepared to put in their totally breastfed babies' mouths is a pacifier. This age-old device, evolving from a small cloth packet of delicate herbs to today's crystal-clear, orthodontically molded nipples, has proven its worth ever since some frustrated mother somewhere must have invented it. Though many nursing mothers initially plan not to use them, their babies often end up with pacifiers firmly in place.

Without entering into the pros and cons of pacifiers, it is advisable for the nursing mother to use them sparingly if at all, lest nipple confusion result. Furthermore, if the baby satisfies his sucking needs with a pacifier, he might not suck enough at the breast and the milk supply may be diminished. In contrast, mothers who serve as their babies' sole pacifiers usually nurse longer.

Weaning

This brings us to the second most frequently asked question: *How long should I nurse my child?* The Talmud states explicitly: "A child nurses for two years, and even four or five if he is weak."[10] Another source gives two years as the average.[11] Stopping prematurely (unless medically indicated) is

---

10. *Ketubot* 29.
11. *Adnei Paz* 17.

not looked upon favorably by our Sages.[12]

Thus, a mother should nurse her child for as long as he and she desire. If she is relaxed and committed, rearranges her priorities, looks after herself, and practices responsive nursing, she will, with God's help, enjoy nursing for a long time. Like all worthwhile activities, the reward is commensurate with the effort, and this is one effort our Sages regarded as particularly praiseworthy.[13]

> *At the age of two, my son was every bit the toddler all the books describe, and yes, he was still nursing! He was quite a chatterbox and loved to imitate his older brothers and sisters, who proudly took over the teacher's role. He got quite a round of applause from them the day he recited the blessing "shehakol" loud and clear before resuming his nursing position in my arms.*

You need not set goals. Take it one day at a time. However long your baby nurses is up to him, and up to you. If, for whatever reason, nursing must be terminated at some point, rest assured that you have done your best.

Modesty

Our nursing practices should reflect our heritage as Jewish women. Modesty and refinement are our crown of glory[14] and a nursing mother should conduct herself accordingly. "A woman who nurses immodestly in front of men other than her husband is liable to a divorce," declare our Sages.[15] With minimal effort, nursing can be carried out discreetly and proceed

---

12. *Ben Ish Chai* II, *Emor* 13, brought down in the name of the Ari.
13. *Yaffe Lalev LeMaharif* 1:240.
14. *Tehillim* 45:14.
15. *Gittin* 89a.

unnoticed under a wide variety of circumstances. Skirts and blouses are comfortable (and fashionable) and can provide adequate air for baby without forgoing mother's privacy.

> *I was preparing to leave the house to visit my mother, who lives a three-hour bus ride away. The baby was strapped to me in the baby carrier. In one hand I carried a tote bag with diapers, in the other my purse. As I did my best to wave goodbye to my husband and three young children, my five-year-old suddenly darted towards the kitchen and called out, "Wait, Mommy, you forgot something!"*
>
> *I was looking around at my baggage, wondering what it was I had left behind, when she came running back with a newspaper.*
>
> *"Here, Mommy, you'll need this newspaper to hide behind if the baby needs to nurse on the bus!"*

This child has been raised in a Torah environment. Even at her tender age, her mother's example of modesty has had an impressive impact, and she has developed sensitivity not only to her mother's needs, but to those of her baby brother as well.

Siblings

Handling a new baby with other children in the house is a juggling act most mothers are familiar with. Here is one mother's story:

> *I awoke with a start. I could hear my two-and-a-half-year-old moving about in her room. Then, in the crib next to my bed, our newborn began to cry. "This is it!" I told myself nervously.*
>
> *Last night, when I returned home from the hospital,*

everything had been perfect. The baby had slept the whole way home and well into the night. Chani was exhilarated at meeting her new sister, who slept through the excitement.

Now I was going to have to nurse the baby in front of Chani. It wasn't so long ago that she had stopped nursing herself. Would she remember? So many mothers had told me about their children's jealousy towards the new baby.

I was prepared for the worst when Chani barged into the room.

"She's awake, Ima," she exclaimed as she peered into her sister's crib.

I took a deep breath.

"Ima, what are you waiting for? She's crying! Don't you know what to do?" she asked. "You have to nurse her—like this." She pointed to herself and indicated to me how to nurse the baby. To Chani it seemed the most normal and natural thing to do.

I heaved a sigh of relief and we proceeded to nurse our baby.

It is often the mother's attitude toward life that provides the older siblings with lessons in loving by giving. To teach her family to be aware of others and to care for one another is the utmost any mother can hope, pray, and strive for, from the moment she brings her new baby home. This is the beginning of her child's education to Torah and mitzvot.

Chapter Seven
Responsive Mothering

The Crying Baby

"Mommy, the baby is speaking Russian!" announced my eight-year-old daughter wearily, wheeling the stroller through the front door.

I nodded. "Okay, honey, you did your best. I'll take over now." I bent over to pick up my wailing child, recalling how my daughter's phrase had become a household expression in our family:

A relative of ours had just arrived from Russia and was staying with us for a few weeks. She was a lovely person, yet we had no language in common. Though we did our best to supply all her needs, she would make unintelligible requests, and we all ended up being frustrated.

Ever since, the children use the term "speaking Russian" when the baby is crying and they don't know what he wants. If he's been fed, changed, burped, walked, bounced, and carried, yet is still upset, then his inability to communicate precisely what he seeks is as frustrating as "speaking Russian" to an English-speaking host.

While trying to soothe a crying baby, it is helpful to realize that he *is* indeed communicating. Crying is his God-given ability to call for attention. He uses it to say: "I have a need." Though we may not always know what it is that he wants, responding to his crying at least conveys our love and readiness to fulfill his desire. Once this message has been communicated to the baby, he may even calm down a bit, at least long enough to give us a chance....

Though it's frustrating to try again and again to soothe a baby who just will not be soothed, the mother should not vent her frustration on him. If she projects anger—through tense hands, a stiff body, and sighs of exasperation—he will become even more aggravated. After all, he, too, is displeased with his inability to articulate his desire. Even we adults sometimes find ourselves unable to express, or even to know, exactly what's bothering us. All the more so, then, small babies, whose nervous system is still so immature.

So, first and foremost, a baby's cries should be looked upon as his only form of speech. The baby is not "out to get you," using every possible opportunity to aggravate and frustrate you. If you have decided that all he wants is attention, well, understand that *for a baby that is a real need*. He may desire interaction and stimulation, simply because he is bored. It's hardly fair to respond with, "Well, go find something to do, then," as one might with an older child. If the mother were to devote just five minutes exclusively to the baby, he might then be at peace for an hour.

The cry for attention may in some cases be due to an underlying, ongoing problem. A woman should always be prepared to reevaluate her mothering practices. Perhaps her nursing sessions are too rushed, or her changing procedure rigid and impersonal. Is the baby left for hours alone in his crib? Has it been a while since he was taken out for a pleasant stroll in the sunshine? Are his needs being tended to while his mother is tensely "getting other important things done" at the same time?

A change in the mother's attitude is often all that's needed to effect a change in the baby. If she can relax and give him the utmost in high-quality attention, she'll be more likely to convince him that the time he spends with her is really *his* time. Once he feels that extra security and trust, his crying spells may become fewer and further between.

For some infants, however, nothing ever seems to work. Such babies cause mothers seemingly endless confusion and dismay. In his book *The Fussy Baby,* Dr. William Sears refers to them as "high-need" infants who share certain personality traits. Twenty-five percent of all babies have many of these traits at some point during early infancy. Besides being light sleepers, they are supersensitive, intense, demanding, unpredictable, overactive, and uncuddly. They awaken frequently and want to nurse very often.[1]

Instead of battling the situation, Dr. Sears suggests that we learn how to bring out the best in these babies. Put aside your displeasure with the lamentable tune he is singing, and *tune in*. That's the best way to reduce his crying.

One of the most fallacious bits of advice a mother can be given is: "Let him cry it out." Here again, our Jewish sources offer us guidelines. "A person must not ignore his child's cries," instruct our Sages, for "women who let their babies cry for a long time while they go about their business will be taken to task for this unacceptable manner of mothering."[2] Clearly, our tradition educates mothers to respond to their crying babies.

> *I used to think baking a really special cake for Shabbat was one of the most important things I could do for my family,*

1. Dr. William Sears, *The Fussy Baby* (LLLI authorized reprint, 1985), p. 2.
2. *Pele Yoetz, Erech Yonkei Shadayim.*

but my husband pointed out that our new baby didn't fully appreciate all my extra effort in the kitchen. Nowadays, we let the bakery do the baking.

Successful nursing means responding to baby's need for nurturance as it arises. Making herself available whenever the baby needs her develops a mother's sensitivity to every individual in her family.

We have too much respect for mothers to suggest that some ignore their baby's wailing out of sheer neglect. This is contrary to the nature of women in general, and mothers in particular. Nevertheless, certain women are convinced, usually by various friends and relatives, that disregarding a baby's crying when "there seems to be no reason for it" is the right thing to do. This is often the attitude of a mother bound by a schedule. "He's not due for another hour," she repeats to herself, trying to block out the sound and justify his being left alone to cry. "When it's time to feed him, he'll be so hungry that he'll nurse better, and that will keep him quiet for the next four hours."

This attitude defeats its own purpose. By the time the "scheduled hour" has arrived, her baby is so worn out from crying that he doesn't have the strength to nurse properly. Though he may suck eagerly for the first minute or so, his energy quickly diminishes and he falls asleep, only to wake up hungry again after a short period. Ultimately, the lack of stimulation decreases the milk flow, frustrating both mother and baby. Although she has only the best of intentions, if this practice continues she will probably end up with a baby who cries often yet never seems satisfied. And although she will blame her milk, the problem resulted from her having interfered with the natural law of supply and demand.

Another hindrance to nursing may be the mother's own anxiety. Emotional upsets within the normal daily range will not affect her milk supply, but ongoing aggravation sometimes inhibits the let-down reflex. For example, a mother who has decided to let her baby cry will probably not be impervious to his distress. The involuntary discomfort she experiences as a result of his crying may influence her let-down reflex. Once she notices she doesn't have enough milk, all that's needed is some advice from a well-meaning friend, and before you know it she has stopped nursing.

The most oft-cited reason for ignoring crying babies is the fear of spoiling them. "He needs to learn discipline," many a mother maintains. And sometimes even grandmothers reprimand their daughters for overreacting to their babies' cries.

We beg to shed some light on this matter, which is one of the most misunderstood issues of child rearing. The importance of discipline is beyond question. However, discipline must suit the age, abilities, and understanding of the child. *Ignoring a baby's cries will teach him nothing.* Far more educational is *responding*. At this stage of development, you don't need to worry about spoiling him, for love has a firmness and discipline of its own. It is not harmful, only beneficial. Imagine how you would feel if you were crying for help and no one came. Then, compare the feelings that would be engendered by a loving response.

Our jet-set society is more concerned with training, mislabeling it "discipline." Modern mothers rush to train their babies as quickly as possible to fit into the adult world. After all, society teaches us that babies are a burden and an inconvenience to their parents, whose "precious time" could otherwise be spent far more productively. By getting them onto schedules right away, introducing solids as soon as possible, and weaning them before they are ready, we try to make them into baby-adults, causing ourselves and our children much sadness and frustration. This egocentric approach only *slows down* the natural process of growth and maturity. It saddles parents with a *really* "spoiled" child.

This is not a Torah perspective. Judaism encourages mothers to devote themselves to a career it holds in highest esteem: mothering. It applauds women like Chanah, who spent years patiently caring for her son. And it instructs us to respect the stages of a child's development.

"Any demand that is beyond a child's developmental age and ability can cause him harm and hinder his progress," says the author of *Alei Shor*.[3] Ignoring an infant's cries in order to teach him patience, tolerance, and respect for clocks and household chores, etc., defies his developmental stage.

In contrast, tending to an infant as his needs arise is a valuable lesson in love. It establishes the foundation for the discipline which will become more and more appropriate as the years go by.

Prof. Michael Lewis, professor of pediatrics at Rutgers Medical School and the top scientist at the Princeton Educational Testing Service, has discovered that the way parents respond to their baby's cries can influence the child's personality. His recent research has shown that a baby who is ignored when he cries feels that he has no control and so develops a helpless view of the world. On the other hand, a baby who gets a response develops an attitude of personal competence. These attitudes can last throughout his life. "Crying should teach the child optimism," Prof. Lewis says. His experiments showed that babies who got a response exhibited more pleasure, more attention, and stayed alert longer, but those who got no response felt powerless and confused, and began to turn off to people and things around them.[4]

Dr. Lee Salk, professor of pediatrics at New York Hospital Cornell Medical Center, firmly claims that children whose cries are answered learn to vocalize well and not to whine or

---

3. *Alei Shor, Ma'amar HaChinuch*, p. 263.
4. *Living and Loving Magazine*, July 1982, p. 15.

whimper. He believes that babies who are left alone for long periods or who don't receive attention when they cry simply tune out. Dr. Salk believes this could be the beginning of what later becomes adult depression. He also notes that cultures that pay a lot of attention to a crying baby have infants that develop faster.[5]

A fussy baby who has spent most of the day in his mother's loving arms is not an emblem of incompetent mothering. Rather, this is evidence of her sensitivity, of her willingness to stop, listen, and tune in. Putting the people in her life, especially the tiny, helpless ones, before the things is what makes her a good mother.

> *It was one of those days. The dishes were piled high in the sink, the toys were strewn all over the floor, and after much humming, walking, and talking, my fussy little one finally fell asleep in my arms. After laying him down in his crib I set about "attacking" the day's mess.*
>
> *It's amazing how different the dishes are from my little baby. They waited quietly all day to be washed and weren't any the worse for it. My baby, on the other hand, would truly have "spoiled" had he been left to cry while I washed the dishes and mopped the floor.*

This attitude can help dispel frustration and give mothers a sense of pride, worth, and satisfaction. The resulting joy shared by both mother and child unites them in the unique gift of love bestowed upon them by God. A happy mother will naturally impart her cheerfulness to her baby. As our Rabbis state: "A nursing mother delights in her child and causes him delight, singing and cooing to him, and making him happy."[6]

Since baby's crying is his way of communicating, we should appreciate his letting us know that some need must be met.

---

5. *Living and Loving Magazine*, July 1982, p. 15.
6. *Tzeidah Laderech* 1:4, chap. 14.

Beyond the physical discomforts which a mother can easily tend to, such as hunger and a soiled diaper, and the emotional needs such as attention and security, ongoing crying may indicate a further problem.

In one case, a baby's medical problem came to her mother's attention only because she responded to her baby's crying and tuned in carefully:

> *One of my twins would nurse happily only on the right side. Every time I switched her to the left breast she cried. The pediatricians and doctors I turned to were as perplexed as I. None of their suggestions alleviated the difficulty.*
>
> *I finally consulted a chiropractor, who discovered that the baby had a twisted spine that caused her intense pain when she lay on her right side. Thank God, the "mystery" was solved and her condition treated successfully. She now nurses normally on both sides. Though her constant crying frustrated me, I am grateful to her for "letting me know."*

Sometimes a baby's non-stop crying presages something that will ultimately give his mother pleasure. Instead of wringing her hands in despair, wishing that he would just keep quiet for a while, she should try to soothe him, remembering that sometimes good things come only with difficulty.[7]

> *I once found myself resenting my first baby. He cried non-stop for three days. Nursing helped calm him, but I was at my wit's end with fatigue and frustration. On the fourth morning, just as I was about to consider putting him up for sale, my son gave me a big smile that recaptured my heart. It was then that I discovered something marvelous had taken place right under my nose while I was busy fretting.*

---

7. *Avot* 5:28.

There it was, staring me right in the eyes, his first tooth! I have since learned to appreciate a baby's crying for what it is: a means of communication.

Patiently tending to a crying baby is a mother's responsibility, one for which she is well-equipped. No other occupation is considered more worthy of her attention. Even her pursuit of spiritual fulfillment should not come at the expense of caring for her children, since caring for them *is* itself a spiritual pursuit: she is raising the children God has entrusted to her.

One Yom Kippur eve in Berditchev, the entire congregation was anxiously awaiting the arrival of the saintly Rav Levi Yitzchak. Though the hour was late, no one would even consider beginning "Kol Nidrei" without him. However, the revered rabbi was nowhere in sight.

No one imagined that at this very holy hour, Rav Levi Yitzchak was in a small hut rocking and soothing a crying baby. He had been passing by the hut on his way to shul when the loud wails of an infant had reached his ears. Since the door was locked, he had climbed through the window.

"The mother is unaware that tending to a baby takes precedence over davening, even on Yom Kippur," he thought to himself.

It was only a while later that one of the congregants spotted the saintly Rav through the window. Rushing back to fetch the mother he related his discovery to the astonished congregants

"How could I possibly beseech God's mercy while a Jewish child was crying so pitifully?" Rav Levi Yitzchak later explained to the congregants who accompanied him to shul. Before beginning the Yom Kippur prayers he raised his hands towards Heaven and exclaimed: "O, Master of the universe, have mercy on Your children, the Jewish people, just as I had mercy on that little baby."

Chapter Eight
Coping with Difficulties

Throughout my first pregnancy, I read many books about childbirth. Time and again I came across the term "natural childbirth." In my naiveté, the word "natural" registered in my mind as "easygoing."

Well, if there was one lesson I learned, it was that even a "natural" labor and delivery is hardly an easygoing experience! Nevertheless, as I gaze upon my beautiful little baby, I know that it was well worth the effort.

This lesson became part of my breastfeeding experience, as well. Though nursing my baby is the most natural thing I could do, it is not always so smooth and simple. Still, as he smiles back at me in love, I know that all we have gone through together was worth it.

In this chapter, we discuss situations that may create difficulty, confusion, or doubt during a woman's nursing career. We hope that despite all obstacles, nursing mothers will gain the strength and determination to continue, knowing that in the end they will never regret their effort.

Before suggesting how to overcome difficulties, we would like to stress one general rule: Most disturbances that develop while nursing are *temporary* and will pass with proper treatment, which is usually quite simple and practical. A nursing mother should not become overwhelmed and stop breastfeeding. It is our hope that this chapter will provide useful medical information to nursing mothers, encouraging their commitment to breastfeeding despite the possibility of brief discomfort.

Sore Nipples

The nipple is a sensitive area, and women commonly experience extreme soreness at the onset of nursing. But the baby's sucking toughens the nipples and the pain disappears fairly soon. The soreness is most acute when the baby latches on, then subsides after the "let-down" of milk. Once the baby is sucking steadily, you will be able to relax and enjoy the feeding. You may be tempted to stop before let-down occurs, or just as it's beginning. But without the baby there to nurse, the increased milk flow can further aggravate the nipples.

Suggestions for sore nipples

* Make sure that much of the areola is in the baby's mouth, as well as the nipple. This will prevent him from "chewing" on the delicate nipple area since he will be putting most of the pressure from his lips and gums on the less sensitive areola.

* Before each feeding, apply a hot water bottle to the breast or sponge it with warm water. Heat treatment hastens let-down, thus limiting the discomfort that precedes it. You can also massage the breast to bring on let-down.

* Let your nipples air-dry after feedings. In a discreet place, at an angle by an open window, you can benefit from the healing properties of the sun while maintaining your standards of modesty. Another way to allow air circulation is by inserting small tea strainer cups between nipples and bra.

* Between feedings, apply drops of your own milk to sore nipples. This remedy has proven even more effective than pure lanolin or ointments made with vitamin A, D, or E.[1]

* Feed the baby as soon as he "calls." An infant who is left to cry is apt to suck much harder when you finally sit down with him. Responsive nursing is a good idea for other reasons, too, as explained in the previous chapter.

* Never pull the nipple out of the baby's mouth lest you bruise it and cause further soreness. Gently reduce the suction by inserting your small finger in the corner of his mouth.

* Check your nursing position. When the baby is positioned incorrectly, the angle from which he is sucking sometimes puts unnecessary pressure on the nipple. By positioning him properly, the pain can be alleviated. The baby's head should be in the crook of your arm, with your hand supporting his bottom. He should be turned on his side, facing you, with the nipple directly in front of his mouth.

* Change your position at each feeding. Sit up for one, lie down for another, or try holding the baby in the football position (his body "tucked" at your side with his face looking up at you as he latches on). By changing positions, you are distributing the pressure of your baby's sucking all around the nipple area. This can take some of the stress off the painful spot and hasten its healing.

* Don't hesitate to contact a trained breastfeeding counselor or lactation consultant. She is trained to recognize incorrect positioning and faulty sucking. In addition to her expertise, her reassurance and encouragement can make all the difference. She will keep you from falling prey to the despair that sometimes accompanies temporary discomfort.

---

1. Lawrence, *Breastfeeding: Guide for Medical Profession*, p. 194.

Dwindling Milk Supply

You may erroneously conclude that your milk supply is dwindling because you notice that your breasts seem less full. This does not mean that your supply is decreasing. Rather, the breasts have simply adjusted themselves to the demand, producing the amount of milk your baby requires.

Similarly, if your baby no longer falls asleep peacefully after each feeding, this, too, does not necessarily indicate a lack of milk. Perhaps he is becoming more interested in his surroundings and is seeking more stimulation, not more milk.

It is also common for babies to go through sudden growth spurts, during which they simply need more nourishment. Do not take his appetite as a sign that your milk is inadequate for him, and that other foods should immediately be introduced. Regard his vigorous sucking as his way of "putting in an order" for an increase in supply. Nurse him more often and your supply will indeed grow.

When a woman's milk supply has in fact dwindled, she should not panic. More often than not, this is a result of fatigue, inadequate diet, insufficient liquid intake, or tension. Remember the general rule: This is a *temporary* situation.

To replenish her supply, nursing counselors recommend the "24-hour plan," in which she delegates her household duties to others for one day so that she can rest, eat, and drink well. While she is taking it *very easy* for these 24 hours, the baby should be allowed to suckle as much as he likes. The "miracle" of this simple yet sure advice has been experienced by overjoyed nursing mothers time and again.

> *I am so happy I took those 24 hours off. I was on the verge of giving up nursing, even though I dreaded the thought of having to prepare and warm bottles. That one full day of total rest made many future days of joyful, easy breastfeeding possible.*

Breast Infections

A swelling of the breast, a painful lump, or a red spot accompanied by tenderness may indicate a plugged milk duct. Essentially, this means that the milk is collecting because its flow is inhibited. If these symptoms appear, along with fever, weariness, achiness, or an overall "under the weather" feeling, it may mean the onset of a breast infection.

Suggestions for dealing with breast infections and plugged ducts

* Begin treatment immediately. Breast infections don't disappear when ignored, as many nursing mothers know from experience.

* Don't stop nursing![2] Unfortunately, this is often the advice nursing mothers are given. Plugged milk ducts or infections are often caused precisely by prolonged lapses in between feedings. The milk surplus resulting from a cessation of nursing will lead to engorged breasts and sore nipples. It could easily have been given to the baby, thus emptying the breast and bringing relief.[3]

When an infection has developed, it is even *more* important to empty the breasts frequently, so do not hesitate to nurse often! Express the milk if the baby is not nursing enough to keep the breast empty. If only one breast is infected, nurse the baby on that side first, when he sucks most vigorously. This will ensure that the infected breast is sufficiently emptied.

Don't worry about transmitting the infection to the baby. Studies have shown that it will not harm him. Usually, only the breast tissue is infected, not the milk itself. If organisms in the breast infection do survive in the milk, they will be broken down by the hydrochloric acid in his stomach, with no ill

---

2. Lawrence, *Breastfeeding: Guide for Medical Profession*, p. 207.
3. Riordan, *A Practical Guide*, p. 155.

effects. Besides, there are plenty of antibodies formed in the milk to protect the baby from infectious bacteria.[4]

To sum up, since keeping the breasts empty hastens healing and alleviates pain, and since nursing through an infection does not harm the baby, the obvious thing to do is: nurse frequently! Sudden weaning is an emotional as well as a physical shock to mother and baby, and an ailing mother is definitely in no position to deal with more stress. Moreover, it causes breast engorgement, prolonging the infection and intensifying the pain.

* Apply heat. Hot showers or baths, and hot water bottles or pads, promote healing and soothe discomfort.

* Loosen any clothing that constricts the body, and avoid tight bras. When at home, remove your bra entirely for a few days or try a different style or size, because pressure on the milk ducts can cause them to close. A fuller, deeper cup is often helpful in this respect.

* Get plenty of rest. As with many illnesses, total body rest is one of the most effective treatments. Rest is essential to any nursing mother, especially during illness.

* Eat, drink, and think positive! While a mother must obviously be provided with a nourishing diet to rebuild her strength and fight the infection, it is of even greater importance for her to maintain a positive attitude in spite of her discomfort. An ailing mother tends to "wean" herself away from nursing, especially if infections recur, so she should muster all her commitment, devotion, and determination in order to continue. She must reaffirm that *nursing is the best way to feed her baby.* A telephone call to an understanding, knowledgeable breastfeeding counselor can work wonders.

*If the condition persists, consult a doctor who appreciates your commitment to nursing and who is experienced in

---

4. LLLI, *The Womanly Art*, p. 243; Stanway, *Breast is Best*, p. 150.

these matters. Many physicians refrain from prescribing antibiotics to a nursing mother unless absolutely necessary, knowing infections generally clear up without them when the above measures are taken. Sometimes, large doses of vitamin C are prescribed instead. If, in fact, there seems to be no alternative to medication, don't panic. Many medicines will not harm a nursing baby. Contact a lactation consultant even while you are seeing a doctor.

* Do your utmost to prevent breast infections from recurring, as they sometimes do when a local infection is ignored amid signs of apparent improvement. Make sure to continue treatment until healing is complete.

* Check your general health. If you are feeling run down and overtired, go for a checkup, including a blood count. Perhaps it is anemia. Most doctors suggest taking vitamins and iron throughout lactation, just as in pregnancy.

Remember that vitamin supplements are not meant to replace your daily diet. Get into the habit of eating well. Sometimes mothers have to be reminded to sit down and eat real meals. Junk foods are not real foods. Drink plenty of liquids as well, and be sure to include fresh fruits, vegetables, and whole grains in your diet. Seek advice from an expert in nutrition if you are not sure what a healthy diet entails.

Some women get breast infections more often than others. If you're one of them, ask yourself:

* "Am I overdoing things? Too much housework? Pushing myself too hard outside the home?"

* "Am I generally happy? If not, what can I do about it?"

* "Do I relax whenever the opportunity arises?"

After a long history of breast infection throughout the years that I nursed six children, I did not have to be convinced to opt for bottle feeding when my seventh was born. As the doctor injected me with the "drying up" treatment, he congratulated me on my "wise" decision. Even my pro-breastfeeding husband agreed that this was the only choice.

During my three-day hospital stay, all went well. My baby was bottle fed and I tried to rest—but there was a gnawing in my heart that was hard to ignore. It robbed me of my peace of mind, even though everyone told me I was doing the right thing.

I arrived home with our baby late Friday afternoon. The tumult that followed finally died down as I lit the Shabbat candles. It was only then that I realized that no one had bought baby bottles! The ones we had were unsterilized and their nipple holes were too large. While I frantically tried to figure out what to do, I recalled that another woman in the hospital had changed her mind after receiving the injection to dry up her milk, and had been told by the doctor that, yes, she could nurse anyway. It seemed the only option for me at this moment.

I gathered my little one in my arms in that close embrace, which I had agonized over denying him, and proceeded to nurse. The delight on his face dispelled momentarily all my worries about the infections that were sure to come.

I nursed this baby for a year and a half, the longest I have ever nursed, and unbelievably, I did not have a single infection!

I sometimes look back, as I light Shabbat candles each Friday evening, on the Shabbat that "compelled" me to nurse. It led to the most rewarding nursing experience I have ever had.

Intense Milk Flow

Some nursing mothers have such an intense milk flow that their babies tend to choke and sputter. The milk flows so quickly that the baby has difficulty dealing with the gush. He also suffers discomfort from all the air which he swallows as a result. Some suggestions:

* In a sterilized container, collect the first spurts of milk, and begin nursing once the milk has stopped flowing so fast. (If you have no need for the collected milk, you can donate it to a milk bank.)

* Douche the breast several times a day with cold water, or give it a quick splash prior to every feeding.

* Try to restrict the flow by gently applying pressure to the areola with your first and second fingers.

* Feed the baby in an upright position, propping him up on a pillow to prevent air bubbles from forming in his stomach.

* Rest assured that this problem will probably disappear when your nursing becomes better established and your milk flow adjusts to your baby's needs.

Inverted Nipples

Truly inverted nipples are rare. This is when the nipples go in when pressure is applied to the areola area. Even in this situation, however, women can nurse their babies successfully.

Flat nipples are more common, yet their shape often improves during pregnancy. Women can promote this improvement by occasional "shaping exercises" throughout the pregnancy. Once or twice a day, they should gently draw out each nipple and roll it between thumb and finger.

After birth, if the baby is having difficulty latching on, a mother can use a nipple shield for the initial latching on. This soft, rubber protrusion cups the areola area, enabling the baby to latch on easily. Once the milk flows, flat nipples become overted and the shield can be promptly removed for the entire duration of the feed.

As a rule, the baby's vigorous sucking is the best treatment for flat or inverted nipples. A nursing mother with this condition should muster extra patience and perseverance. As usual, expert guidance from a lactation consultant is most helpful.

Baby's Preference for One Side Only

Sometimes a baby develops a preference for one breast over the other, even after nursing beautifully for months.

* Don't worry that he is not getting enough. There is an abundance of evidence from nursing mothers who have undergone mastectomies on one side—and those who have breastfed twins, giving each one side only—that one breast can do the job as well as two.

* Try offering him your other breast while keeping him in the same position. Perhaps for some reason he feels more comfortable lying on one particular side.

* Allow him to nurse from the preferred side first. Perhaps the milk on this side "lets down" more quickly, or maybe the flow is more intense. After he has satisfied his initial hunger, he may be more willing to nurse from the slow-flowing side.

* If the baby absolutely refuses one side, express milk from it regularly to avoid engorgement and maintain the milk supply. Keep offering the rejected breast at each feeding. Babies usually come around to nursing on both sides eventually.

When Baby is Ill

> *When my fifteen-month-old was hospitalized with a very high fever, the doctors decided to put her into a cold bath for at least twenty minutes. She was very unhappy and pleaded with me to come out. As it was of utmost importance that she stay in the tub, I racked my brains for a way to keep her there. Finally, while my husband guarded the door, I leaned*

over the tub and nursed her. The thankful look on her face made me thankful to God for the gift He had given us both, enabling me to comfort my little girl.

Any nursing mother can testify to the comfort and security breastfeeding provides. The ability to offer relief to a sick child is greatly appreciated by both him and his mother. Even where other foods are undesirable, nursing is almost always beneficial. Many mothers have nursed their way through a wide range of children's diseases, bringing comfort to their children along with the nutrients and immunological factors. As detailed medical situations cannot be covered in a book of this nature, a doctor and a lactation consultant should be consulted.

Jaundice

Even normal, healthy, full-term babies can develop physiologic jaundice on the second to fourth day after birth. In most cases it disappears in about a week, often untreated. Jaundice is quite harmless and leaves no aftereffects.[5]

One of the best ways to deal with this type of jaundice is simply to nurse frequently right from birth. Colostrum is especially important in helping the baby discharge the meconium (first stools of the newborn), thus preventing bilirubin re-absorption. This helps rid the baby of the jaundice.

Mothers are often instructed in the hospital to give their newborns bottles of water (usually sweetened) to flush out the jaundice. However, Dr. Lawrence Gartner, who has done extensive research on neonatal jaundice, reports: "Water or supplements given to newborns in the first four days do not affect the degree of jaundice."[6] Frequent nursing is a much

---

5. Riordan, *A Practical Guide*, p. 205.
6. LLLI, *The Womanly Art*, p. 225.

better idea, as it increases the flushing of the bilirubin via the meconium.[7]

The most common treatment for jaundice is light therapy. But it is not so well known that sunlight serves the same purpose as those "bililights" in the hospital nursery that isolate a baby from his mother. The infant should not be put in direct sunlight, however. He can lie exposed in a bright room and your nursing sessions will not be disturbed.[8]

If artificial light therapy must be used, insist on minimum interference with nursing. Nurse frequently, even waking the baby if he tires easily under those lights. Remove his eye covers when you nurse, cuddle him, and provide plenty of contact. Holding and stroking him while he is under the lights is highly recommended as well. He'll need that extra love and security.

Thrush

Thrush is an infection that appears as white patches in the baby's mouth and as redness and inflammation on the mother's nipple and areola. Oral thrush is caused by *candida albicans* or other strains of yeast. It thrives in the warm, moist areas of the baby's mouth and on the mother's nipples. A mother who has been nursing comfortably and suddenly develops extremely sore nipples can suspect thrush.

Examine the baby's mouth for telltale signs, consulting a doctor if need be. Your doctor may prescribe medication, or you can try this highly effective, natural means of treatment:[9]

* For baby: Dissolve a level teaspoon of baking soda in a cup of water and firmly swab the baby's mouth. After each feeding, sweep the inside of his cheeks and gums, especially

---

7. LLLI, reprint no. 84, June 1982.
8. LLLI, *The Womanly Art*, p. 228.
9. LLLI, information sheet no. 19, 1980.

his tongue. Use a fresh cotton swab each time and change the solution every day.

* For mother: Bathe the nipples in a vinegar solution after each feeding—one tablespoon to one cup of water. Use a light coating of Vaseline to prevent dryness.[10]

* The nursing mother should expose her nipples directly to the sun twice a day (discreetly, of course). If direct exposure to the sun is impossible, sunlamp treatment is also helpful. (Get explicit instructions for its use from a breastfeeding counselor.)

* Most important: Keep nursing! None of the various treatments suggested requires you to discontinue breastfeeding.

Nursing While Taking Medication

Dr. Sumner J. Yaffe, professor of pediatrics and pharmacology at the University of Pennsylvania School of Medicine, has issued a thought provoking statement: "The question is not whether a medicated mother should be allowed to nurse, but whether a nursing mother really needs to be medicated...."[11]

Nowadays, it is common knowledge that nursing mothers should avoid medication, just as pregnant women do. In some situations, however, medication may be imperative. If so:

*Verify the danger of the medication before hastily concluding that you must stop nursing. Doctors often advise a mother to wean her baby "just to be on the safe side," but weaning is a major decision and should not be looked upon casually. Many mothers have undergone difficult weaning experiences in order to "protect" their children, only to discover later on that it was totally unnecessary. It could be that the drug is completely safe but the doctor has no time to check.

10. LLLI, *The Womanly Art*, p. 242.
11. LLLI, information sheet no. 21, 1978.

Most lactation consultants keep themselves well-informed and up-to-date on drugs commonly prescribed for breastfeeding women. Contact a counselor and ask her.

* Make inquiries about substitute medication. Frequently, there are other drugs that are equally effective but harmless to the baby. Don't hesitate to seek options. After all, abrupt weaning can be far more difficult than a few phone calls to a doctor, pharmacist, and breastfeeding counselor.

* Find out when to take medication so as to minimize its absorption into the milk. Sometimes it is best taken before the feeding, sometimes directly after. Drugs vary in their absorption patterns and this information can be very helpful.

* If you are considering the option of weaning, get expert advice before making a hasty decision. As mentioned, weaning can be a traumatic experience for mothers and babies both. The mother can develop a breast infection and the baby can become utterly inconsolable. This tension will certainly not promote a mother's well-being. Weigh the pros and cons. Nursing mothers whose medical condition permitted them to choose, never, in our experience, regretted the decision to forgo drugs. And those who took the time to find out whether they could go on nursing despite the drugs were forever thankful that they did so.

Emotional Difficulties

Most situations discussed have dealt with physical conditions and their relation to nursing. There are, however, emotional aspects to be considered, as well. One woman relates:

> *When my first child was born, I found the very idea of nursing terribly repulsive. On my doctor's advice, I forced myself to do it anyway, stubbornly persisting for five months and hating every minute of it.*

> *Finally, I couldn't stand it any longer and stopped cold turkey. At that point it became apparent that my son was extremely allergic and the doctor told me that I had saved his life by nursing. He looked askance at my decision to stop.*
>
> *When he advised me to nurse all my future children, as allergies run in our families, I broke down and cried. I simply hate nursing.*
>
> *My second child is now eleven weeks old. I clench my fists, tense my body, and nurse her. As far as I'm concerned, nursing is not that beautiful, fulfilling experience all the books describe.*

This mother faces an unenviable dilemma. Perhaps a few ideas might encourage her:

Nothing God created should be regarded as repulsive.[12] Nevertheless, we all have our likes and dislikes, which contribute to the colorful nature of human life. A mother who dislikes nursing should seek out people who understand her feelings and respect the effort she is making for the sake of her child. She should also read as much as possible about the benefits of nursing, to fortify her resolve.

We ask her to bear in mind that one's reward is commensurate with one's difficulties. If she can triumph over her emotional difficulties in this instance, she will develop the inner strength to overcome a wide variety of other challenges. It is our fervent hope that she will succeed.

Post-Natal Depression

Another condition that bears mention is *post-natal depression*. Many a husband finds himself at wit's end when his wife returns from the hospital depressed, weepy, and unable to cope. He can't comprehend how she can feel so low at a joyous time like this.

---

12. Ramban, *Iggeret Hakodesh*, chap. 2.

It is important to stress that her reaction is not unique. Childbirth has both physiological and psychological effects; the hormonal changes sometimes cause mood swings and extraordinary sensitivity. Besides, the responsibility of tending to a new baby is both physically and emotionally taxing.

The best way for a husband to deal with the "baby blues" is to offer support, empathy, and understanding. He, usually more often than anyone else, can build up his wife's self-confidence by complimenting her on her mothering skills. He must protect her from any unwelcome comments and dismiss any discomfort she may feel about accepting housework help. It's up to him to see that she is taking care of herself. By encouraging breastfeeding, he is doing his wife, his family, and himself a great service. The mothering hormone, prolactin, a valuable by-product of nursing, can go a long way towards restoring her emotional equilibrium.

A mother undergoing post-natal depression should not be condemned and rebuked, as this will only worsen the situation. All those around her should be loving, warm, and supportive, for such an environment is conducive to a speedy recovery. If the blues do not clear up and serious depression sets in, professional help *must* be sought.

Something that is often overlooked is the effect of a poor diet on a mother's state of mind. Her well-being is directly related to her nutrition, and if she is depressed, the duty of preparing healthful meals for herself cannot be left up to her. So the first step taken should be to make sure a nursing mother is eating properly.

> *I found myself so irritable by the end of my fourth week at home with our third child that I thought I needed to see a doctor. The excitement of the brit milah had passed, the guests had left. I was "merely" tending to the needs of the baby and my two older children now. So why should I feel*

so low? While discussing it with my husband, I happened to mention that I never seemed to find time to eat breakfast till lunchtime.

Every morning for the next two weeks, I found an appetizing breakfast laid out for me on the kitchen table.

I was saved a trip to the doctor.

Chapter Nine
Managing in Special Situations

The Premature Baby

Though breastfeeding benefits all babies, it is especially advantageous to the premature infant. The vital nutritional components of breastmilk, as well as the loving act of nursing, are of great importance to his healthy development. Breastfed "preemies" thrive and can often be discharged from the hospital sooner than their bottle fed peers.[1]

Due to its low fat and carbohydrate content, breastmilk is digested quickly and easily, without burdening the baby's immature kidneys. The efficient breakdown of fat in his tiny body enables him to utilize it to the fullest.

Research suggests that the breastmilk of a preemie's mother adjusts to his special needs, for it contains more protein than the breastmilk of mothers whose babies were born at full-term.[2] This is a blessing for the delicate and vulnerable premature infant. It betters his chances of survival and increases the peace of mind of his mother, who wants so desperately to help him.

Also of great importance is colostrum. Premature infants

---

1. LLLI, information sheet no. 13, Dec. 1980.
2. Lawrence, *Breastfeeding: Guide for Medical Profession*, p. 312.

are more susceptible to infection than full-term babies and are in dire need of its natural immunizing properties.

A mother's awareness of these benefits will help her persevere in establishing a nursing relationship with her premature baby. She will need that extra measure of determination: A pre-term baby has an immature sucking reflex and it may take some time for him to nurse normally. His interest in suckling, as well as his physical need for food, is also less developed. It is therefore crucial for the mother to maintain her milk supply until he has grown large enough to suckle more vigorously. To do so, she must empty her breasts at short, regular intervals. The expressed milk may be stored and fed to the baby from a bottle until he is strong enough to suck properly from the breast.

Expressing milk

The basic law of "supply and demand" applies to any method of emptying the breasts. The more they are stimulated, the more milk they will produce. There is no hard and fast rule governing the expressing of milk: every woman must discover the frequency, position, and manner that best suit her. She may want to begin with two- or three-hour intervals, increasing or decreasing the length of time between sessions to maintain the desired supply.

Expressing milk is not difficult. Once you become accustomed to it, you will be surprised at how easily it can be mastered.

Cup your breast in your hand, with your finger just behind the areola. Placing your thumb on top and another finger underneath, supporting the breast, squeeze your fingers together rhythmically while pressing back towards the breast wall. Do not slide your fingers along the skin. Rotate your hand around the breast in order to tap all the milk ducts radiating from the nipple.

After you've worked on one breast for up to five minutes, start on the other. Then, do each side once more. This repetition stimulates the milk flow.

Other helpful hints:

* Get plenty of sleep. A well-rested mother produces more milk.

* Choose a comfortable spot and position.

* Stimulate the "let-down" reflex by taking a warm shower, massaging the breasts and thinking about the baby.

* Drink plenty of fluids.

* Wash your hands thoroughly before expressing milk. There is no need to wash the nipples; a daily shower is sufficient. Nor is it desirable to clean them before expressing, lest you wash away their natural antiseptic secretion.

In the case of the premature infant who is not nursing, the expressed milk he is fed by bottle or tube (or even spoon) must be properly stored. Sometimes the hospital provides containers. If not, you can use your own, as long as they are sterilized. Plastic containers are preferred because some important immunological components of breastmilk may adhere to a glass receptacle.[3]

If the expressed milk is to be used within twenty-four hours, it may simply be refrigerated. When in transit, pack it in dry ice. The milk can be stored in your freezer for up to two weeks.[4]

Nursing a premature infant means that the mother will be making frequent trips to the hospital. Though this can be a strain on her, especially since she herself is just recuperating from the birth, it is a blessing in disguise. The physical contact nursing entails is crucial to both of them. Stroking, caressing, and holding the baby serves to develop her mater-

---

3. LLLI, information sheet no. 13, Dec. 1980.
4. ibid.

nal instinct until her tiny infant can come home with her. And it provides the baby with the comfort and security he must have—something the busy nursery staff cannot always offer.

By tenderly caring for her premature infant, the mother is building up her emotional and psychological resources, and her trust and faith in God. The birth of a premature baby can be accompanied by anxiety, depression, and even misplaced guilt. The mother must face the possibility of a loss. Many mothers who have gone through this experience say that giving of themselves to the baby—visiting, nursing, touching, talking, and telling him how much they love him—helped them cope with the difficulty much better.

A mother who is having trouble breastfeeding should nevertheless do her very best to nurse the baby herself. Though milk banks are available, breastmilk varies somewhat from mother to mother and her own milk provides him with the best immunization possible. By avoiding stored milk, there is less chance of infection. Furthermore, many hospitals insist that donated milk be sterilized. The heat destroys vitamins, desirable bacteria, and other important components, and alters protein composition.[5]

Meanwhile, she should gladly accept any household help that's offered, as well as any emotional support from those around her. She will never regret the effort she invested during this critical period, for someday she will see with just how much joy she was repaid.

The Lact-aid nursing supplementer

If her baby's sucking reflex is not strong enough to bring on the milk, a mother may find the lact-aid most helpful. The lact-aid is a simple device designed to encourage the baby's suckling while providing him with milk, regardless of imme-

---

5. LLLI, information sheet no. 13, Dec. 1980.

diate breast response. It contains a closed plastic bag with a very thin tube attached. The bag is filled with milk (preferably mother's own, expressed) and the open end of the tube is placed at the nipple. As the mother offers the breast, she inserts the tube along with the nipple. Satisfied with the steady flow from the bag, the baby suckles happily, thus providing the breast with the stimulation it needs. Milk production should begin soon, gradually building up to the required level. This device is more practical then giving the baby supplemental bottles, as it avoids nipple confusion and actually stimulates milk production.

Whatever method a mother is using to maintain her milk supply, she should put her premature baby to the breast often, to encourage his sucking. He may even have to be woken up sometimes, since he may be more interested in sleeping than in nursing. Relax and prepare to take your time. Since he is not very strong, he'll need plenty of patient cuddling and coaxing. He may not be able to suck well for more than a few seconds at a time.

To avoid tiring him, express a little milk until you have a let-down and then put him to the breast. If he has been fed by tube or bottle, he may become confused. Reassure him, handle him gently, and keep offering the breast by brushing his cheek with the nipple so his head turns toward it.

In the beginning, you may find yourself able to put him to the breast only once or twice a day. Look upon this as a good start, knowing that as time goes on, nursing will become better established. Once the baby is nursing well, discontinue all use of bottles or any other artificial nipples. This will prevent nipple confusion and stabilize the nursing relationship. Consulting a lactation consultant will also provide, in addition to helpful information, much needed encouragement and support.

When our fifth baby was born prematurely, it took all of us a while to get used to the idea of a pre-term infant.

"Gosh! He looks like a robot wired up to all those machines," exclaimed my seven-year-old when we visited our new baby in the hospital.

"I wish there were some place on him to pat," complained my little four-year-old, searching for a spot among his tiny body tubes.

As patiently as I could, I explained their brother's sensitive situation. I needed double the amount of patience just for myself. For weeks I expressed my milk, keeping up the supply. Looking back, I honestly don't know how I managed, both physically and emotionally. Yet I know I couldn't have had it any other way. I was determined to nurse this baby.

Today, six months later, while I was gently rocking and nursing him, my ten-year-old daughter sat down beside me and said softly: "Ima, he looks so happy. After all those tubes and wires—he likes being 'wired' up to you best of all!"

If the baby could have expressed himself, I dare say he would have wholeheartedly agreed.

Relactation

Relactation is the process by which a mother re-establishes her milk supply several days, weeks, or even months after previous lactation has ceased. (In fact, some mothers have been able to establish a milk supply for their adopted babies without ever having given birth.) It is possible because the sucking of the baby stimulates milk production, though it is a process that takes time and patience.

If a woman could not nurse her child for some time, or has weaned her child only to discover that he cannot tolerate formula, or if she simply changes her mind and decides she wants to nurse, relactation can be a God-sent solution.

My baby was a healthy, robust three-month-old when I stopped nursing her, but soon after weaning she developed severe diarrhea and diaper rash. We went from doctor to doctor and tried formula after formula, but nothing helped for long. This went on for almost two months. Finally, a leading pediatrician told us, "There is only one solution, and that is mother's milk."

Sure enough, the donated mother's milk did the trick: for the first time in two months my baby fell asleep peacefully after a feeding and the diarrhea disappeared. Yet we spent all our time running around in search of her next meal, until a La Leche League leader told me about relactation. She warned me it would take time and patience, but it could be done.

I started off using the donated milk in a "Lact-aid," and slowly but surely my milk supply returned. Within two weeks I was nursing my baby again, and she was on the road to a full recovery.

The Working Mother

This issue is quite controversial, with almost as many opinions as there are mothers. We will discuss it in light of the experiences many mothers have shared with us. It is our hope that every mother, and those who nurse in particular, will seriously weigh the pros and cons of this delicate issue.

I was a working woman. My self-image was that of someone who contributes to the human work force. The upcoming birth of my first baby filled me with many thoughts and considerations, yet not one of them concerned my job. It seemed obvious that I would arrange for baby care and return to work as soon as possible after the birth.

It was only after I discovered motherhood, though, that

I began to realize how much my baby and I both needed and enjoyed each other. I asked myself a question that had never before entered my mind: Do I really need to go back to work? I was taken by surprise at the ease with which I answered: No, not really.

I wonder sometimes how many working mothers are struggling through the day only because they never contemplated the option of staying home with their babies. As for me, I'm glad I stopped to think, and I'm thankful for the choice I made to say home with my baby.

Another woman realized, too, that while the work force out there could manage just fine without her, her baby could not.

I work for an architectural firm and my baby arrived right in the midst of a major project. I planned to take a month off and then return to work for just a couple of months, till we completed the project. At that point I would turn all my energy back to my baby.

"It's okay to leave him in someone else's care for the first few months," I told myself repeatedly. "After all, he really doesn't need that much attention when he's so small. I'll be there all the time when it really matters, when he's older and more aware."

Well, that first month taught me that education begins from day one. Eventually, I decided that I couldn't possibly give up those early months, even for a contract to redesign the White House! "There will always be other architectural structures to create," I resolved, "but shaping and molding the person my baby will become is not something I'll be given a second chance to do. It's not a project that can be assigned to anyone but me."

These mothers were in the position to make a choice. However, others simply must work, whether they want to or not. Even so, an option exists.

> *It must have been a man who coined the term "going out to work." But if it was a woman, it certainly wasn't a nursing mother!*
>
> *I am a member of a group that promotes home-based activities: catalogue shopping, banking by phone, home entertainment, etc. When my baby was born and I realized that I would not compromise on response nursing, I discovered through my participation in the organization that I could still bring in the necessary earnings without leaving the house. Many ideas suddenly became real possibilities. I also found myself in the very supportive company of other nursing mothers.*
>
> *We discovered a wide range of possible businesses. All of them called for determination, commitment, and consistency, traits these nursing mothers seemed to possess in abundance.*
>
> *Another important factor was creativity. As one of my friends put it: "I was as creative as a stone wall until I became a mother. My children brought out the creativity I never dreamed I had. Rainy-day activities, inexpensive outdoor excursions, Purim costumes, making up lullabies... these and many other parental pursuits developed a new resourcefulness within me, which served me well when I was setting up my own home-based business."*

Another nursing mother reports:

> *At first I thought it would be impossible to do bookkeeping at home. I need peace and quiet when dealing with numbers, and I didn't think it would work. I discovered, though, that*

the children did allow me a few relatively calm hours. As long as they knew that Mommy was around, they were content. More than my actual involvement, they simply felt secure on account of my presence. Even the nursing baby allowed me my time—for he felt secure that his time would come, too.

A teacher-turned-writer is equally pleased with working at home:

I end up with a larger net income now. Though I earn less because I take on projects at my convenience to allow for plenty of mothering time, my expenses are fewer. I don't have to constantly replenish my wardrobe. I'm less self-conscious now that I'm not facing groups of students every day. I dress in simple, comfortable clothes all day long, saving on dry-cleaning expenses, too. I haven't neglected my appearance and I still enjoy dressing well, but I have discovered just how costly dressing for the job can be.

Still another member of the home-business association:

I was working for a bakery that specialized in parties. We made the most exclusive wedding and birthday cakes you can imagine. Still, under the heavy work load, I never really felt that I was developing my talents to my own satisfaction.

I left my job shortly before giving birth, knowing that full-time mothering was more important to me than professional baking. As those early months flew by, I decided to try my own home-based special occasions bakery. By limiting the orders, I found myself with plenty of time in a relaxed atmosphere, which was conducive to success. As sales increased, I realized that by staying home I had achieved far more than I ever would have in somebody's else's business.

Here are just a few suggestions for directions you may follow in pursuing your career at home:

* Child care. You can care for other children in your home while you are caring for your own. There is an ongoing need for this service in every Jewish community. Whether you open your own nursery or simply babysit, this could be a source of steady income. One woman set up her own agency, gathering information on all available child care and classifying it according to age, hours, terms, cost, etc. For a reasonable fee, she finds suitable child care for her clients and makes all the necessary arrangements.

* Teaching. From tutoring schoolchildren to giving music lessons, organizing aerobics classes or offering Lamaze instruction, there seems to be no limit on what people want to learn.

* Secretarial work. Many firms are more than happy to send work home, thereby saving on office space. Typing, bookkeeping, accounting, and computer programming can all be done at home. It pays to invest in a computer; sometimes the office will share the expense.

* Writing. From creative writing or translating to short articles and books, you can turn your literary talents into cash. One woman offered to make up stencils for grade-school teachers. Demand was so great that she hired two others to help.

* Telephone jobs. Many jobs can be done by phone. If you cannot find one, try creating one, as one woman did: she offered to place seminary girls for Shabbat. The school was pleased to be relieved of this time-consuming job and the woman made many new friends by phoning, not to mention the welcome income.

* Home sales. Whether it's maternity clothes or educational toys, open your own basement shop.

* Get crafty. Sewing, painting, puppet-making, embroidery,

calligraphy—there's no end to the artistic creations people are anxious to purchase. You can sell privately or offer your products to stores and outlets.

* Holiday helpers. Our Jewish calendar provides many opportunities to offer items or services to the public. There is always a market for sukkah decorations, Purim costumes, or Tu BeShvat kits. One woman came up with a money-making idea that originated from a personal frustration.

> *I always ended up with a large amount of expensive olive oil after Chanukah, because it is sold only in bulk. So one year I bought one large container of oil and several small bottles, filling each one with enough oil for one menorah. These economical bottles sold very well and brought in a handsome profit.*

It seems as if the list is endless, allowing for much variety and individuality and, of course, allowing a breastfeeding mother the comfort and satisfaction of response nursing.

Despite all these options, though, many women must work outside the home. But with effort and planning, they can still continue nursing. Some suggestions:

* Investigate the possibility of taking your baby to work with you. Depending on their professions, some mothers have been able to nurse on the job.

* Consider taking baby plus babysitter.

* Try putting off your return to work as long as possible. Many a nursing mother has been surprised at the understanding attitude of her boss, who agrees that she take another couple of weeks or months off.

* If you can find a babysitter near your work place, pop in frequently to nurse. Otherwise, perhaps the babysitter can come visit you with your baby during your break.

* Adjust your work hours so that you are not away from

home for long periods. For example, one mother had to put in twelve hours of office time a week. She was able to change her schedule from two days of six hours each to four days of three hours, thus minimizing the feedings she would miss.

Any missed feedings will obviously call for expressing your milk. Since we discussed this issue at the beginning of this chapter, we will just mention a few additional points:

* Nurse responsively for as long as you can. Don't spend precious nursing sessions training the baby to drink your milk from a bottle, preparing him for your future absence. When the time comes, he'll catch on soon enough. In the meantime, give him all you can of yourself.

* Organize yourself for expressing milk at work in order to maintain your supply and avoid engorgement. Dress in a way that makes expressing comfortable and easy. If your office has no refrigerator, keep a thermos or some dry ice on hand.

* Always leave milk for the baby. Even if you plan to be gone for just a short time, don't count on it. Unexpected events have a way of cropping up just when you're in a hurry to get back to a hungry baby. Traffic jams and subway snares are all too familiar to all of us.

* Adopt a positive attitude towards nighttime feeds. Though we address this bit of advice to all nursing mothers, it is particularly important for those who go out to work. On the run all day, somehow managing to fit in feedings, these women can come to appreciate that special time at night alone with their little babies who may have been waiting for their attention all day.

Unlike those hurried daytime feedings when the mother is in a rush to get to the office, the baby at night is fed when *he* is ready. There are no other pressing matters to disturb. Instead of sighing wearily at the sound of his call, relax and view these nighttime "appointments" as a heaven-sent opportunity to enjoy the sheer pleasure of cuddling a warm, responsive baby. It is not just an exchange of nutrition, it is an exchange of love.

A nursing mother who goes out to work is especially susceptible to discouraging comments like: "For goodness sake, you look so washed out. You should really stop breastfeeding!" Of course, you can expect to feel tired. What conscientious working woman who runs a home and cares for her family's needs does not get tired? Single working women, too, constantly feel fatigue. However, there is an enormous difference between the weariness that results from the job and the tiredness that comes from doing something of the utmost importance to you and those you love most—when you know that your rewards will last a lifetime.

Breastfeeding Twins

> *It can be done! Though everyone, from the hospital staff to my husband's great aunt twice removed, insisted that it would be impossible, I nursed my adorable twin girls for fifteen months, the first eight months without any other supplements or food. I simply could not imagine any other way; their four older sisters and brothers were all breastfed babies (and toddlers!). I constantly reminded myself to look upon them as two individual children who should not miss out just because they happened to be born together.*

This woman's positive attitude can serve as an inspiration to all nursing mothers of twins. A tremendous amount of effort is required to succeed. The mother of twins may even find herself too busy to enjoy them in the beginning, but as many mothers of multiples confirm: "They will never cease to delight you."

Breastfeeding twins requires equal amounts of self-confidence and humor. Confidence boosts milk production and humor helps keep the days of "breastfeeding marathons" in proper perspective. You can be sure that your great effort will be rewarded with even greater delight.

Suggestions for a nursing mother of multiples

* One or even both babies may need extra hospital care and might not be able to nurse immediately. To boost your milk production enough to meet both babies' needs, express your milk regularly and don't give up any night feedings.

* Coordinate feeding sessions:

Option a: Use both breasts for both babies at every feeding.

Option b: Use one breast for each baby, alternating at every feeding.

Option c: Nurse the hungriest baby at the fullest breast.

Option d: If you have "assigned" each baby a breast for every feeding (or he prefers it that way), make sure to alternate position so that he receives adequate visual stimulation.[6]

* Simultaneous feeding is helpful, if the babies cooperate. Most mothers do not nurse their twins simultaneously at every feeding—only sometimes. Using pillows, you can experiment with different positions until you find one that works best:

Option a: Place one baby in the traditional nursing position, with the other's head on the first baby's abdomen—football position. In this position the baby faces you while his body is tucked

---

6. Riordan, *A Practical Guide*, p. 56.

under your arm. Pillows are helpful to avoid arm strain.

Option b: Place both babies in the traditional position with their bodies crisscrossed or supported by your thigh. Usually twins feed well when they are touching each other.

Option c: Place both babies in the football position.

Option d: Lie on your stomach, propped up on your elbows and supported by pillows.

* Take care of yourself. As a mother of twins, you will learn quickly to think double about anything that pertains to your babies' needs. Apply this to yourself as well. You will need an extra measure of rest, household help, and nutrition. Remember that by taking care of yourself, you are taking care of your babies as well. Do not hesitate to consult a breastfeeding counselor and other mothers of twins. Their support can prove invaluable.

Nursing and Pregnancy

Many medical authorities hold that, generally speaking, there is no need to wean a child if his mother becomes pregnant.[7] Some women even nurse right through pregnancy and continue nursing two children after the birth. This is called *tandem nursing.*

If there are no medical contraindications, when a woman becomes pregnant she should decide for herself whether or not to stop nursing. Avoid the trauma of abrupt weaning. Take your time and do what suits both of you. Sometimes the baby will wean himself early in the pregnancy, sensing a mild change in the taste of the milk. In other instances, he stops nursing as the pregnancy progresses, noticing a reduc-

7. Stanway, *Breast is Best,* p. 193.

tion in the milk supply. Still other babies wean toward the end of the pregnancy, when the milk changes to colostrum. If your baby has a strong desire to nurse despite the effects of pregnancy, you have nothing to worry about, as long as you're resting enough and your diet is adequate.

One word of advice: when tandem nursing, always feed the younger baby first. Whereas the older child is eating other foods in addition to breastmilk, the little one is totally dependent upon you for his nourishment. You in turn *must* make sure your diet is nourishing and adequate, and includes foods high in protein.[8]

Weaning

"Education begins at day one."[9] Just as nursing is one aspect of that education, so is weaning. "Educate your child according to his way" instructs the wisest of all men, Shlomoh HaMelech.[10]

Just as babies cut their first tooth, begin to crawl, attempt to walk, and start verbalizing coherently at different ages, some nurse longer than others. Some children have very strong sucking impulses, while others have an intense need for closeness and contact. Still others may have latent allergies or other physical problems that prolong their need to nurse.

Our Jewish sources discuss the right time to wean. Ideally the child should wean himself. It is written that one should not wean a baby before his time unless there is a specific reason for doing so.[11] "The duration of the halachic status of *mesuleket damim*—the woman who does not menstruate—

---

8. Riordan, *A Practical Guide*, p. 321.
9. *Alei Shor, Ma'amar HaChinuch*, p. 263.
10. *Mishlei* 22:6.
11. Rav Chaim Vital, *Eitz Chaim*, sec. 288: *Nitzotzin*.

corresponds to the average nursing time of two years. A child who so desires may nurse for three, four, or even five years for a sickly child."[12]

Of major concern is that the mother should nurse willingly and comfortably. A woman who is discontented with her nursing career should make every effort to develop a more positive attitude.

If a woman feels, for whatever reason, that she must put an end to the nursing relationship, rather than wait for the child to do so, we suggest that while she should not offer him the breast, she shouldn't refuse him either. Try at all costs to avoid a "cold turkey" weaning, for it can be as hard on your system as it is on your baby's emotional and physical health. If you resolve to take your time and don't expect miracles overnight, there are many ways to distract your little one and interest him in the world beyond nursing. Exercise as much patience as you can and shower him with loving closeness. Your baby will gradually get used to the idea that though his nursing career has come to an end, a childhood filled with his mother's love has only just begun.

> *My baby was nine months old and his sister was two-and-a-half, and she was still nursing together with him. He grew ill and the doctor prescribed antibiotics. After a few days, suddenly my nipples started hurting terribly. When I inquired, a lactation consultant told me that antibiotics can cause thrush, which can spread to the nipples in the form of cracks.*
>
> *I was nursing my feverish baby every hour, and when my little girl asked for her share I explained that the frequent nursing was bothering me because of the cracked nipples. She surprised me with her answer: "Ima, I don't have to*

12. *Ketubot* 60a.

nurse if it bothers you, just feed the baby. I am already a big girl!"

With that she was weaned. I will never forget that precious moment.

Chapter Ten
The Beginning

My great-grandmother was celebrating her ninetieth birthday. Gathered around her were her daughter (my grandmother), her granddaughter (my mother), and myself, a new mother of a six-week-old little girl.

It is not often that one finds five generations of mothers and daughters sitting around the table, and I could not help feeling quite emotional about the gathering.

But it was my great-grandmother herself who summed up my thoughts in a short speech she made.

"My daughters," she said, "I look at you all and I see myself at different stages of my own life. I've been through them all and I have a message for you:

"Being a mother is the most challenging, most difficult, but also the most rewarding, and most fulfilling job you will ever be employed to do. Do not underestimate it. But on the other hand, do not feel guilty or despair over the mistakes you have made or may make. As none of us are perfect, there will always be room for improvement. Even to this day I pray to God that I should find the right words to speak to you with. You and your husbands are creating masterpieces. But never forget that you have another partner who will

> *complete the picture for you. It is not up to you to complete the work.*
>
> *"You begin, do your very best, and trust in Hashem to do the rest."*

"And she nursed her son until she weaned him, and she brought him up with her—and she brought him to the House of God."[1] And she said, "For this child have I prayed and God has granted my request which I asked of Him, and I also have lent him to God all the days...."[2] Chanah's prayer is the prayer of every Jewish mother, the prayer of a devoted mother who has done her very best for her child. She has nurtured him with love, and when the time comes she gladly hands him over to a life of Torah and mitzvot.

---

1. *I Shmuel* 1:23-34.
2. ibid. 1:27-28.

Appendix
Breastmilk, Breastfeeding, and Jewish Law[1]

Shabbat and Yom Tov[2]

1. To interest a passive baby in nursing, a mother may express a bit of milk directly into his mouth, but not into a cup or container.
2. A woman who is very uncomfortable because of her engorged breasts may express her excess milk into the sink, onto the ground, or onto a cloth. She should not use any cloth that she normally would not want to get wet, since she may come to wring it out. Though expressing milk is generally forbidden on Shabbat, our rabbis have ruled leniently if a woman is in pain, and if the expressed milk is not used.

   If it is difficult for her to express, she may use a

---

1. Although the laws in this section have been thoroughly checked by rabbinical authorities, a Rav should be consulted whenever a specific question arises.
2. The laws in this section are based on *Shemirat Shabbat Kehilchatah* 36:19-22, and have been written with the permission and guidance of the author, Rav Yehoshua Neuwirth.

manual pump, emptying it frequently so as not to accumulate a sizeable amount of milk.

3. Concerning a baby whose mainstay is his mother's milk, if he cannot nurse normally, or if he is hospitalized and his mother must provide fresh breastmilk daily, she is permitted to express her milk into a container because the baby may be endangered if fed other milk. This ruling even applies to a baby who has not yet become accustomed to his mother's milk. Breastmilk is considered a baby's natural food and one should not take the slightest chance of endangering him by feeding him anything else.
4. In the case of inflamed nipples that must be treated on Shabbat, remedial cream should be applied to cloths beforehand. A woman may then apply these cloths on Shabbat. (They should be properly protected from possible contamination.) She is also permitted, when necessary, to take medicine or receive injections to prevent breast inflammation.

Yom Kippur[3]

5. Nursing mothers are obligated to fast on Yom Kippur.
6. Women who have given birth within one week of Yom Kippur must consult a Rav concerning their obligations on Yom Kippur. In addition, if a nursing mother's baby depends on her for nourishment and she will not have enough milk for him if she doesn't drink, she must consult a Rav for instructions.

   Most nursing mothers find that if they drink a lot

3. The laws in this section are based on *Shemirat Shabbat Kehilchatah* 39:10-17.

before the fast they are able to fast and nurse without experiencing any difficulty.

7. If a nursing mother feels that if she attends synagogue services she will become weak and find it difficult to fast, she *should not* expend her energy by going to shul. Better she should stay home and fast than go to shul and then need to drink.

Tishah B'Av and Other Fast Days[4]

8. Nursing mothers are obligated to fast on Tishah B'Av. A woman who has given birth within a month of Tishah B'Av, and any nursing mother who finds it difficult to fast, should consult a Rav for instructions.

9. Nursing mothers are not obligated to fast on the minor fast days—the fast of Gedaliah, the tenth of Tevet, the fast of Esther, and the seventeenth of Tammuz—even if they suffer no discomfort.

   A nursing mother who wishes to fast on minor fast days is permitted to do so (except within a month of giving birth). There is, however, no necessity to try to fast. A nursing mother who is weak should not fast and one who grows weak from fasting is not permitted to do so.

   Nursing mothers who are not fasting should not eat or drink for enjoyment, but only to sustain themselves and their babies.

---

4. The laws in this section are based on *Torat Hayoledet* 47:1-3, 48:1-4, and 55:2, by Rav Yitzchak Zilberstein and Rav Dr. Moshe Rothchild.

General Laws

10. Breastmilk is kosher and pareve, but may be drunk by someone who is not nursing only from a cup.[5]
11. Although pareve food normally may be warmed in a meat pot, breastmilk should not be, lest an observer mistake it for cow's milk.[6]
12. A healthy child may continue nursing until he is four years old. A weaker child may continue nursing until he is five.[7]
13. A child over the age of two who has weaned himself for over seventy-two hours should not resume nursing unless it is necessary for his well-being. But if the child was forced to stop nursing because of an illness, he may start again even after many days have passed. A child under the age of two may resume nursing even if he weaned himself for a month or more, but he should not nurse after turning two, unless it is necessary for his well-being.[8]
14. A mother may study Torah and recite any blessing or prayer, with the exception of *Shemoneh Esrei,* while nursing.[9]
15. A husband may study Torah and recite blessings and prayers in a room in which his wife is nursing, but only if no parts of her body which are normally covered are exposed.[10] If she is not completely covered, he may still study Torah and recite blessings if his entire body is turned away from his wife.[11]

---

5. *Shulchan Aruch, Yoreh Deah* 81:7.
6. Ibid., 87:4.
7. Ibid., 81:7.
8. Ibid.
9. *Shulchan Aruch, Orach Chaim* 74:4.
10. Ibid., 75:1.
11. *Mishnah Berurah* 75:1.

16. Women may study Torah and recite blessings and prayers in a room where a mother is nursing, even if she is not completely covered.[12]

12. *Mishnah Berurah* 75:8.

Women seeking guidance in mothering through nursing and mothers wishing to be trained to offer assistance to other mothers in any country may obtain further information from the international offices of Jewish Marriage Education:

JME
P.O.B. 18103
Jerusalem 91180